D1391948

EARTH HEROES

Lily Dyu

EARTH HEROES

ILLUSTRATED BY JACKIE LAY

nosy
crow

First published in the UK in 2019 by Nosy Crow Ltd
The Crow's Nest, 14 Baden Place
Crosby Row, London SE1 1YW

www.nosycrow.com

ISBN 978 1 78800 852 5

Nosy Crow and associated logos are trademarks and/or registered
trademarks of Nosy Crow Ltd

Text copyright © Lily Dyu, 2019
Cover and chapter opener illustrations copyright © Jackie Lay, 2019

The right of Lily Dyu and Jackie Lay to be identified as the author
and illustrator of this work has been asserted by them in accordance
with the Copyright, Designs and Patents Act 1988.

All rights reserved. This book is sold subject to the condition
that it shall not, by way of trade or otherwise, be lent, hired out
or otherwise circulated in any form of binding or cover other
than that in which it is published. No part of this publication may
be reproduced, stored in a retrieval system, or transmitted in any
form or by any means (electronic, mechanical, photocopying,
recording or otherwise) without the prior written permission of
Nosy Crow Ltd.

Nosy Crow does not have any control over, or any responsibility for,
any author or third-party websites referred to in or on this book.

A CIP catalogue record for this book is available from the
British Library.

Printed and bound in the UK by Clays Ltd, Elcograf S.p.A.

Typeset by Tiger Media.

Papers used by Nosy Crow are made from wood grown in
sustainable forests.

1 3 5 7 9 10 8 6 4 2

For my much-loved friends
Chris and Rhona D'Arcy
L.D.

To my forthcoming child, and to all the
future children of the world
J.L.

CONTENTS

INTRODUCTION

THE FUTURE
IS IN
OUR HANDS

Half a century ago, humans stood on the moon for the first time. Perhaps the most important image from the moon missions wasn't of astronaut Neil Armstrong taking his first step onto the grey lunar desert, but actually one taken a few months earlier, on Christmas Eve, 1968. It was then that the *Apollo 8* mission sent the first manned spacecraft to orbit the moon. The team were searching for future lunar landing sites, and one of the astronauts took a photo as our planet appeared over the moon's horizon. This picture became known as Earthrise. It shows the dull, lifeless surface of the moon and behind it our beautiful blue planet, alone in the blackness of space. The astronauts remember it as being the most breathtaking sight, filling them with love and longing. It was the only thing in space that had any colour, and it struck them that they'd come almost a quarter of a million miles to photograph the moon, but it was the Earth that was really worth looking at.

I grew up with dreams of looking upon the Earth from space. As a teenager, I wanted to be an astronaut and, instead of pictures of my favourite bands, my room had a poster of a NASA astronaut floating above the Earth. Winter evenings were spent stargazing from the garden, picking out my favourite constellations. I wasn't really an outdoorsy child, and I only discovered nature in my twenties when I took up running. Muddy trails led me to forests, rivers, mountains and clifftops, with their rich abundance of life. I fell in love with the natural world; it was where I felt most at home and running in the wild filled me with an intense connection to the living environment around me.

I have learned that astronauts, too, feel a deep connection with all life on Earth once they see our planet from space. Below them is a world without borders – a miraculous swirl of land, ocean and clouds. They realise that humans are just one species alongside other creatures on Earth and are shocked to see our planet's fragility and vulnerability. Our atmosphere, nurturing all life, looks like a paper-thin shell. It is the only thing protecting us from deadly cosmic radiation and the hostile environment of space, and the only thing preventing us from becoming like other lifeless planets in the solar system.

Humans have created an environmental emergency here on Earth, dangerously warming our atmosphere. Climate change is the biggest threat humankind has ever confronted. And we have already destroyed so much of our astonishing natural world. We need to act now so we can continue to share our one home planet with each other and all life. Scientists say it is achievable, but we are running out of time. In October 2018, the United Nations Intergovernmental Panel on Climate Change issued a special report saying that we have 12 years to limit warming to 1.5 degrees Celsius. It argues that if temperatures rise beyond this, many of the negative effects of climate change will be irreversible. Our beautiful world will be changed forever.

Faced with such a shocking statement, it's easy to think that there's nothing we can do. News headlines often focus on negative stories, so we rarely hear about any of the good things that are happening. But there are in fact countless people doing amazing things to protect our planet and conserve nature. These are ordinary people, most of whom aren't looking for the spotlight, and in this book you will meet *Earth Heroes* that you have heard of and many more you have not, whose stories show that we can all make a difference.

From Chewang Norphel, the engineer building artificial glaciers in Ladakh, to Doug Smith, the biologist returning wolves to America, and from Stella McCartney, the designer creating sustainable fashion, to Melati and Isabel Wijsen, the schoolgirls saving Bali from plastic pollution, these *Earth Heroes* show that one person, no matter how small, really can change the world. And if nations can work together to put people into space, then imagine what we could achieve together for Planet Earth if only we tried.

As conservationist and tiger defender Bittu Sahgal tells people who ask how they can help protect nature, "Be who you are and do what you do best."

Everyone matters. The future is in our hands.

Lily Dyu
September 2019

GRETA THUNBERG

GRETA THUNBERG

THE SCHOOLGIRL WHO SPARKED A REVOLUTION

The forest was burning. Enormous orange flames curled around tree trunks and climbed into the canopy. The heat was intense and smoke filled the air. A hundred volunteer fire fighters – students, teachers and holiday-makers – had come from Jokkmokk, the nearest town, to help. As Greta watched the drama unfold on her television screen, they pointed hosepipes at blazing trees and blackened stumps. Above the crackle of flames and thud of falling branches, she could hear the thrum of a helicopter overhead, as its pilot desperately dropped water bombs to douse the flames.

It was July 2018. It had been a freakishly hot summer in Sweden, with a drought and the highest temperatures recorded in over 260 years. Wildfires had raged uncontrollably through the country's forests. Jokkmokk is famous for its winter market, but even this area of Lapland at the Arctic Circle had not escaped the fires, the largest of which tore through an area the size of 900 football pitches. In Greta's home city, Stockholm, it had been the hottest summer since records began, with many days exceeding 30 degrees Celsius.

A month later, Greta sat at her kitchen table making preparations. She thought about the key facts people should know about global warming and, choosing her words carefully, neatly wrote out a stack of flyers. Then on a board she painted the words 'School Strike for Climate'. Her parents tried to dissuade her, but the next morning, instead of heading off to school, she stuffed the flyers and some schoolbooks into her rucksack, jumped on to her bike and pedalled to the Swedish parliament building. She sat down outside, propping her sign up against the wall. People hurried by on their way to work, clutching briefcases and sipping from coffee cups. But if they noticed the slight girl with long brown pigtails, they didn't stop to find out more.

Greta was skipping school to protest about climate change. All summer, she had followed news of Sweden's wildfires and the heatwave that had killed hundreds of people across Europe. In 2015, Sweden had been one of 197 countries that signed the Paris Climate Agreement; each country had agreed to reduce their greenhouse emissions so that the rise in global temperature could be limited to less than two degrees Celsius, but little had changed since that time. Without action, children like her would grow up in a world dangerously affected by climate change, and yet nobody seemed to be doing anything about it. She had no choice but to act. Greta would strike from school until Parliament made the urgent changes to laws needed to meet the Paris targets.

This moment of protest didn't appear from nowhere. Greta had been building up to it for the last seven years. She lives in Sweden's capital city, along with her younger sister. Her mother is an opera singer and her father, an actor, stays at home to look after his daughters. Growing up, Greta learned piano and ballet, and loved being outdoors – horse riding and walking the family's dogs. Before her climate strike, she had just been a normal schoolgirl, if a little quiet and shy – the girl at the back of the class who was afraid to speak up.

Greta was eight when she first learned about climate change. Her teacher had shown her class a film about melting Arctic ice, starving polar bears and plastic in the oceans. As she watched, Greta cried. And when her classmates went back to their games, she could not forget what she had seen.

Greta started to read everything she could about the problem. She discovered that global warming is causing droughts, floods, extreme heatwaves and forcing people to leave their homes. Human actions are also destroying wildlife and their habitats. She was shocked that the world has known about climate change for 30 years, but instead of treating it as an emergency, adults didn't seem to be taking it seriously. TV programmes and newspapers weren't talking about it, and little had been done to try and stop it. What kind of world would she live in when she grew up?

Aged 11, feeling hopeless about the planet's future, Greta became depressed. She stopped going to school, she stopped eating and lost 10 kilograms in weight. She also stopped speaking to anyone apart from her family. Greta was off school for a year while her parents took care of her. During that time, she learned that she had Asperger syndrome, which means she has a different way of seeing the world compared to most other people.

While at home, she eventually told her parents about her worries about the environment. Sharing her fears made her feel a little better. After that, Greta would not stop talking to her parents about the climate crisis and showed them books, articles, films and reports she had found. Her parents grew to realise that they'd never really taken the issue seriously before. By then, Greta had already become a vegan, and had stopped shopping for new things. Soon her father became a vegetarian and her whole family stopped travelling by plane. They started to cycle to get around and replaced their car with an electric one. Seeing her family change made Greta realise that she could make a difference. It helped to lift her out of her depression, and she decided to devote her life to fighting climate change.

Greta returned to school, where she joined a climate action group. Inspired by school strikes in America to protest against guns, someone suggested they could have a school strike too. Greta loved this idea but no one wanted to join her, so she left the group and decided to strike alone.

On the first day of her protest, Greta sat outside the parliament building from 8.30 a.m. to 3 p.m. –

the whole school day. She posted pictures on social media and from the second day people started to join her. Newspapers were soon reporting her story. Passing politicians told her she was wasting lesson time, but she told them adults had wasted 30 years by not acting against global warming. Others said she should go back to school and study science so she could find a solution to climate change, but she told them that it had already been found: greenhouse gas emissions had to stop. All that was needed was for people to wake up and change.

Greta skipped school for three weeks, up until Sweden's elections in September. After that she decided to continue her strike every Friday, even through the harsh Swedish winter. In ice and snow, wrapped in a yellow raincoat, ski trousers and a woolly hat, she sat outside Parliament. People had ignored her when she first started her protest, but now adults, as well as students, travelled to join her. Greta's story spread around the world and soon students in other countries were inspired to hold their own 'Fridays for the Future' school strikes too.

In autumn 2018, Greta stood for the first time in front of thousands of people. It was a climate change rally outside the European Parliament. Her parents had worried about their shy daughter taking the stage, but Greta insisted on going. That day, she gave a perfect speech in English, her second language. Her father was so proud that he cried.

Since then, Greta has spoken all over Europe. Her parents drove her to London so she could address thousands at an Extinction Rebellion protest. She has given a TED talk that has been watched by millions on YouTube. And, unlike the leaders of the countries she has visited, Greta matches her words with actions. She took a 32-hour train journey to talk to world leaders in Davos, Switzerland, while others arrived by private jet. And to give a speech in New York, she travelled by racing yacht because it was the most environmentally friendly way to cross the ocean.

In her speeches, Greta has warned the world's leaders that they're stealing their own children's futures through inaction. She doesn't want them to offer people hope. In fact, she doesn't want them to feel hopeful at all. She wants them to feel the same panic and fear she feels each day when thinking about the climate crisis. And then she wants them to act.

Juggling schoolwork with saving the planet takes a lot of time and energy. Greta gets up at 6 a.m. to get ready for school. Homework, interviews and writing speeches can mean working 15-hour days. However, she always catches up on missed lessons and is still near the top of her class. The importance of what she's doing gives her the strength to keep going. And she believes that, rather than being something she would want to change, her Asperger syndrome has actually helped her activism. It has allowed her to see problems clearly, and meant she was happy to begin her strike alone.

If not stopped, climate change will affect people all over the world, and could lead to wars, as drought and crop failure force people to leave their homelands in the search for food. To recognise her work, Greta has been nominated for the 2019 Nobel Peace Prize, the youngest person ever to be nominated for this very important award.

In March 2019, seven months after Greta first sat down in front of Sweden's parliament, she was there again, but this time alongside 20,000 students marching and chanting slogans. That same day, 1.6 million students in 125 countries, from Australia and Uganda to Japan and America, left their desks to take part in over 200 peaceful marches in the Youth Global Climate Strike for the Future. Greta's lone protest has grown into a global movement.

Greta will strike outside Parliament every Friday

until Sweden acts on the promises it made in the Paris Agreement. And only when our leaders wake up and listen to the scientists will she and other young people gladly return to school. In the meantime, she says that if children can make headlines all over the world by skipping school one day a week, imagine what we could all achieve together if we tried. But if there is one thing that Greta's incredible story proves, it's that we each have the power to demand change – and that we are never too small to make a difference.

MOHAMMED REZWAN

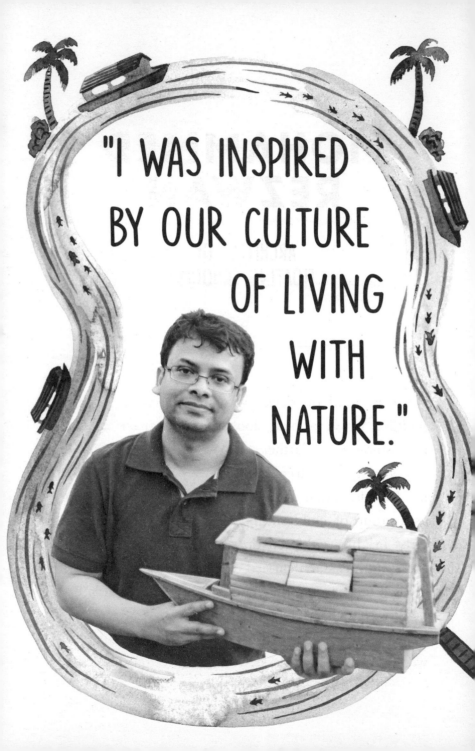

"I WAS INSPIRED BY OUR CULTURE OF LIVING WITH NATURE."

MOHAMMED REZWAN

ARCHITECT OF
FLOATING SCHOOLS

Rezwan stood on deck, watching the river. A man paddled by in a boat, looking for a place to cast his fishing net. Further along the bank, a teenage boy swung off a tree into the water to cheers from his friends. Then Rezwan heard excited chattering as a group of children appeared from the bush. The girls' brightly coloured dresses looked like jewels in the sunshine. Each carried exercise books under their arms. One by one, they climbed the ramp on to the boat, with a chorus of, "Good morning, Mr Rezwan!"

Inside, the children took their seats. Another 20 pupils were already at their desks, in rows of five on either side of the boat. At the front of their floating classroom the teacher was writing a lesson on the blackboard. There were shelves full of books at the back. Rezwan pulled up the ramp and followed them inside. There was a roar as the engine started and the boat pulled away. Just one more pick-up before they could start the morning's lessons.

The children were in north-west Bangladesh, on board their floating school. Here in the monsoon season, between June and October, homes and villages are cut-off as roads disappear under water. Then, many children cannot get to school and sometimes the schools themselves are flooded and closed. The floating schools enable children to go to school all year round. These were the brilliant idea of Mohammed Rezwan, or Rezwan as he likes to be known.

Rezwan grew up here, in a village called Shidhulai, living with his mother, brothers and grandmother while his father worked away in the capital city, Dhaka. With a brick house, they were luckier than many of their neighbours whose homes had mud walls, but during the monsoon even their corrugated-iron roof let in water. In this poor, rural area, there were few schools and no libraries or health clinics. Their village had no electricity, and although in the evenings the family lit a kerosene lamp that gave out a dim light and unpleasant fumes, they rarely ventured outside after dark.

Rezwan's school was nearly 90 minutes away on foot. Girls were not allowed to go to school, because their parents worried about their safety on the long walk, and they were often expected to stay at home and help their mothers. In Bangladesh, one-third of girls are married by the age of 15 and two-thirds by 18. Because his family had a boat, Rezwan was able to go to school throughout the monsoon season, but many of his friends and relatives were not so lucky. Some gave up on school altogether.

Throughout his childhood, Rezwan had seen people struggle bravely through floods and terrible cyclones, picking themselves up and rebuilding their lives time after time. Despite suffering poverty and hardship, they kept smiling and showed great resilience and hope. He believed that, if only they had more resources and support, these people could achieve wonderful things, and this made him want to do everything he could to help them. After attending college in Dhaka, Rezwan studied architecture because he wanted to design schools and clinics for his community, but he quickly realised that those buildings would simply end up under water. This is because, despite producing far fewer greenhouse gases than the world's rich nations, Bangladesh is the country most affected by climate change.

Bangladesh lies on a huge river delta where three major rivers meet the sea. The entire country is low-lying, and flooding is now more frequent and severe due to climate change. To the north, in the Himalayan mountains, glaciers are melting, bringing more water into the rivers, along with sediment that settles and makes them shallower. Land beside rivers is washed away as they get wider. To the south, sea levels are rising and submerging the land. During the monsoon season, one-fifth of the land in Bangladesh is flooded, but at worst this can be up to two-thirds of the country. It's estimated that, if the situation continues, the country will permanently lose up to one-fifth of its land under water.

Bangladesh is the most densely populated country on Earth, with a population the size of America's squeezed on to an area half the size of the UK. Every day, people are forced to leave their flooded homes because they can no longer work or grow food. Wildlife such as the rare Bengal tiger is affected as their mangrove forest habitats are drowned, pushing them into populated areas, where they sometimes attack humans. Many displaced families move to the country's overcrowded capital city, where they can end up living in slums. It's predicted that around 20 million climate refugees will leave Bangladesh in search of a new home by 2050.

Rezwan saw the effects of climate change and knew that he had to find a different way of approaching his building designs. He thought of the boat builders he had often watched as a boy, and he had an idea: if children couldn't go to school, then the school should come to the children. He would build floating schools.

When he'd finished his studies, Rezwan's friends and family tried to persuade him to get a well-paid architect's job instead, but his mind was made up. All he had was $500 and an old computer, but he set up a charity called *Shidhulai Swanirvar Sangstha* ('self-sufficient Shidhulai' in Bengali). Although he wrote to hundreds of organisations, no one wanted to help fund his idea, so he decided to find another way. He organised the collection of waste, like plastic and glass, from the communities near his home and sold it to recycling companies. It took four years, but Rezwan was eventually able to raise enough money to buy four old traditional boat hulls, and he transformed these into school boats using local materials and the skills of local workers. With the help of a boatman and teacher, also from the community, his first floating school was launched in 2002.

Villagers were sceptical at first. They had never heard of a floating school. On the first day, only one child attended. By the end of the week, there were six. And by the end of the month, they had 30 pupils. As people saw the benefits, more wanted to send their children to the school, including many parents of girls. So Rezwan added more boats.

News of his project spread around the world and at last, in 2004, he got his first international funding – from an American organisation, Global Fund for Children. This was followed by further grants. The money allowed Rezwan to put more of his innovative ideas into practice.

Firstly, he added solar panels to the boats so that they could power computers inside (something that even the government schools did not have). This also meant they could light the classrooms in the evenings to provide classes for children who worked during the day. The solar panels generated more electricity than the schools needed, so Rezwan designed solar lamps which families could use at home, allowing children to study in the evenings.

The floating schools taught children until the age of 12, including lessons about conservation and the biodiversity – or varied wildlife – of their country's rivers. But Rezwan saw that there was a thirst for knowledge amongst teenagers, so he added floating libraries installed with computers with internet access. Here, young people could meet, borrow books and learn to use the computers, connecting them with the world outside their villages.

Rezwan wanted to train adults, too, especially women. He added double-decker boats to his fleet, which travelled from village to village to deliver training in new skills such as sewing, sustainable farming and adapting to climate change, along with information on women's rights. These boats were also used for movie nights, with educational films and other programmes projected on to a sailcloth screen. Villagers watched from the riverbank and, for the first time, people young and old could gather together after dark, instead of staying indoors.

These poor communities were also in need of accessible health care. So Rezwan designed mobile floating clinics, with an on-board doctor, free health education and medicines. He also designed a playground boat, where children could use swings, slides and monkey bars when there was no land to play on.

Rezwan had an ingenious solution to the problem of flooded farmland too. He invented floating farms – structures built using old plastic drums – with duck coops to provide eggs and meat, fish pens, and barrels full of soil and natural fertiliser to make a floating garden. Here people could grow food such as cucumbers, beans and spinach to feed their families, allowing them to remain in their riverside homes, rather than being forced to move to the city.

Rezwan is proud to have won international awards for his work, including four United Nations awards for his floating school and solar lantern designs and a Bill and Melinda Gates Foundation award for providing access to education and information. He works very hard and still has many challenges to face. Although he doesn't look for praise or fame, some people are envious of his influence, popularity and success. He spends a lot of time trying to raise money for his projects, travelling all over the world to give presentations, which are very often unsuccessful because so many other charities are competing for the same funding. But, like the communities he has dedicated his life to help, Rezwan never gives up. He loves working with his staff and volunteers to make his ideas become reality and, best of all, seeing how they change people's lives.

In the 21 years since he set it up, Rezwan's Shidhulai Swanirvar Sangstha charity has helped half a million people in north-west Bangladesh. Today they have 23 floating schools, 10 libraries, seven training centres, six health clinics, two playgrounds, 10 transportation boats and a fleet of 54 additional boats that are currently only used during the monsoon season, due to a lack of funds. Nearly 18,000 children have attended their floating schools, and many girls who might have married young say that they want to be doctors, teachers or computer engineers when they grow up. Meanwhile, Rezwan is working to extend his floating schools and community services into other parts of Bangladesh and he has helped to set up similar projects in Vietnam, Cambodia and the Philippines.

Rezwan knows there is still a lot more work to do, and his most recent design adds a house to the floating farm structure, where an entire family can live. He sees his country's future as one of floating communities and thinks that Bangladesh has no choice but to prepare for a life on the water. Rich nations need to act urgently to cut their greenhouse gas emissions, but meanwhile his country must find its own solutions. And since flooding will be a problem affecting a billion people worldwide, perhaps soon it will be those other nations that look to this forward-thinking architect, and his tiny, resilient country, for help in adapting to climate change.

STELLA McCARTNEY

"I'M A REAL BELIEVER THAT JUST DOING A LITTLE SOMETHING IS REALLY A LOT BETTER THAN DOING A LOT OF NOTHING."

STELLA McCARTNEY

THE STAR OF EARTH-FRIENDLY FASHION

Beneath the chandeliers and ornate gold ceilings of the Palais Garnier opera house in Paris, a model strode down the catwalk in a billowing yellow dress and grey boots. Fashion fans and reporters filled rows of seats, eager to catch a first glimpse. As she turned, another stepped out in an emerald green jumpsuit and big black boots. Soon a third came onstage in a long blue coat, clutching a matching handbag. Cameras flashed and journalists scribbled notes. Stella watched from the wings, eager to see how her designs would be received. How many of the reporters knew that the boots and bags were made of vegan leather lined with polyester from recycled water bottles, or that some of the dresses were made from man-made spider's silk?

It was spring 2019, and Stella McCartney was showing off her latest collection at the Paris Fashion Show. The famous designer has made gowns for popstars and princesses, and kitted out Team GB for two Olympic Games, but she is probably best known for her cruelty-free and sustainable fashion – that is, fashion that won't damage the planet for future generations. Stella has never been afraid to stand up for her principles.

Stella grew up surrounded by animals on organic farms in Scotland and Sussex. She has two sisters and a brother and is the daughter of Sir Paul McCartney, a member of the Beatles, a world-famous band from the 1960s. Her mother, Linda, was an American photographer who met her father when she photographed the band. Her parents loved animals, but it was only after seeing lambs playing outside the window one evening as they were eating lamb chops that they decided that they didn't want to eat meat any more. Stella and her siblings grew up as vegetarians, although this was more difficult and unusual in the 1970s and 80s than it is today.

Stella sometimes hung out with her parents' famous

friends, but she much preferred spending time with her family at home in the country to hopping on to a private jet to watch her father play a huge concert for thousands of people. Even though she was from a wealthy family, Stella went to an ordinary state school because her parents wanted her to have a normal childhood and to learn the importance of hard work. She often used the name Stella Martin because she didn't want people to always ask, "Are you Paul McCartney's daughter?"

When her parents started a new band called Wings, the whole family sometimes went with them on tour. Stella was fascinated by the outfits the band wore onstage and loved trying on her mum's clothes and shoes. By the age of eight, she knew that she wanted to be a fashion designer when she grew up. Aged 12, she made her first item of clothing – a jacket made of pink fake suede. From then on, she dreamed of having her own fashion label, with stores across the world.

In her teens, Stella did work experience with various designers before going to college in London to study fashion design. She sometimes had disagreements with her tutors as she refused to work with leather, fur or feathers, because she believed passionately that it was wrong to kill animals for their skin. As well as being cruel, using animals in this way also has a huge environmental impact because of the resources – like land, water and food – needed to raise them. And Stella argued that using animal products for fashion was old-fashioned and that it was more exciting to use modern materials in their place.

After graduating, Stella opened a small shop selling her own dresses. But not long afterwards, the owners of a struggling fashion brand, Chloé, asked her to come and work for them in Paris as the brand's Creative Director. She was only 25. Although luxury fashion houses usually make most of their money from shoes and handbags, which are often made of leather, Stella told them she would not use animal products. Some people said that she only got the position at Chloé because of her famous father, but Stella ignored them and worked hard to prove them wrong. Her fresh new designs proved to be a huge success.

Sadly, when Stella was 26, and less than six months after her first fashion show for Chloé, her mother, Linda, died of breast cancer. As well as being a photographer and musician, Linda had become an activist for animal rights – campaigning against the use of animals for food, clothing, experiments or entertainment – and had also started a business selling vegetarian food. Stella had always been inspired by her amazing mother, whose death affected her deeply. It made her more determined than ever to always stand up for her beliefs, and since then she has dedicated many of her collections to her mother.

In 2001, Stella left Chloé and set up her own fashion brand, Stella McCartney. Now she had the chance to really put the environment and animal welfare at the heart of her business. Stella had always wanted her clothes to be beautifully made and long lasting, so they could be handed down from mother to daughter to granddaughter. But what if the fabrics they were made from could be more environmentally friendly?

Stella had been aware for some time that fashion can be very damaging to the environment. It is believed to be the second most polluting industry in the world after energy production. The factories and vehicles involved in making and transporting textiles produce more greenhouse gases than all international flights and shipping combined, while chemicals and dyes from the production of textiles and leather have polluted many rivers worldwide, and every year 150 million trees are chopped down to make fabrics such as viscose.

Many clothes are made from fabrics, like polyester and nylon, that are manufactured using chemicals from oil, and these shed millions of tonnes of plastic microfibres into our environment each year. Growing cotton uses more pesticides than any other crop, and although organic cotton is less damaging, it takes 20,000 litres of water to make just one T-shirt or pair of jeans, and cotton is often grown in countries where water is scarce. Meanwhile, the increase in fast, cheap fashion has resulted in one rubbish truck of clothes being burned or buried in landfill each second, while only one per cent of textiles are recycled.

Determined to put the planet first, Stella finds it exciting to work with innovative companies to find materials that won't harm the environment and are cruelty-free. Stella uses a vegan leather that looks identical to the real thing, and is experimenting with Mylo, a new leather-like material made from 'mycelium' – the roots of mushrooms. Instead of using silk from silkworms, she is using micro silk made from yeast protein. Scientists learned how to make this by studying how spiders spin their webs. All her company's polyester is made from recycled water bottles, while instead of nylon Stella uses Econyl made from fishing nets salvaged from the ocean. Her company's viscose is produced from wood fibre from non-endangered forests, which means that customers can buy a copy of Meghan Markle's famous wedding reception gown made from cloth that started life in a Swedish forest.

Her business has been hugely successful and Stella now has more than 50 stores worldwide, just as she dreamed as a child. These are environmentally friendly too, powered by renewable energy, with wood floors from sustainably managed forests. The mannequins are largely made from biodegradable sugar cane – a substance that breaks down naturally without damaging the environment – and the walls of her flagship London shop are decorated with paper pulp recycled from the shredder in the company's head office. She believes that doing lots of small things can make a difference when it comes to looking after the planet.

After nearly two decades of doing things her way, Stella is working hard to change the whole fashion industry, and slowly but surely those changes are happening. Recently, several famous brands – Gucci, Burberry, Versace, Calvin Klein and Armani – have announced that they will stop using fur, as has London Fashion Week, while Helsinki Fashion Week is now leather-free. Most recently, Stella used her spring 2019 Paris Fashion Week show to campaign for protection of the Leuser rainforest in Indonesia, which is home to critically endangered animals such as rhinos, tigers, elephants and the orangutan.

Stella has teamed up with the Ellen MacArthur Foundation to try to encourage people to reuse clothes by selling them on or by choosing to rent rather than buy outfits for special occasions. They are also working to increase the recycling of unwanted textiles. Alongside her breast cancer charity, Stella McCartney Cares Pink, she has set up an environmental charity called Stella McCartney Cares Green, which shares her experience in sustainable fashion with other brands. In December 2018, she helped to launch the United Nations' 'Fashion Industry Charter for Climate Action' to ask the industry to agree to stop damaging the environment. We don't have long to make these changes, but Stella is hopeful her work will make a difference.

Today, Stella is married and has four children. She loves being a fashion designer and sees her business and employees as her second family. Her rock star dad is incredibly proud of his daughter and is regularly seen in the front row at her shows. Stella has stepped boldly out of his shadow and is leading the way towards an Earth-friendly fashion industry, where care for the planet is at the heart of every new collection.

ROK
ROZMAN

ROK ROZMAN

THE KAYAKER MAKING CONSERVATION COOL

As Rok pulled up his paddle, he could see fish beneath him. Dragonflies darted over turquoise water and a bird flew on to a nearby rock. He whooped with excitement as he steered around a boulder and through some rapids. Rok and his friends formed a procession of 20 brightly coloured kayaks zipping through the gorge. Around them, the forested riverbanks rose to towering cliffs. This was one of the most magical places he'd ever seen.

It was spring 2016. The group was touring the Balkans – a region in south-eastern Europe – to try to stop the construction of 2,700 hydroelectric dams.

That evening they sat around a crackling campfire, eating and drinking and laughing. It was late when Rok crawled into his tent, but he still planned to get up early to go fishing. As he snuggled into his sleeping bag, he thought about their wonderful day, and felt angry that the beautiful river they'd kayaked would be destroyed if plans to build a dam upstream went ahead.

Rok Rozman is a former Olympic rower, biologist, extreme kayaker and now environmental activist. He first fell in love with rivers and nature when he was a child. He grew up in Slovenia close to a river, where his father took him fishing, and he was always outside, exploring and riding his bike, or flying model planes. He loved animals, sharing his room with a pet iguana and raising a raven that had fallen from its nest, and he was a keen birdwatcher.

Rok also excelled at sports. Because he was so full of energy, his parents enrolled him in ice-hockey classes, and he went on to play for the national team. After that he took up rowing and represented Slovenia at the 2008 Olympic Games, aged 20. But while recovering from a back injury he realised that chasing medals didn't make him happy. It felt selfish. So he gave up rowing and went to university to study biology, his favourite subject, followed by a year researching tawny and eagle owls. But he hadn't lost his love of sport, and while at university he swapped rowing for kayaking, travelling all over the world for adventures that included paddling down 20-metre waterfalls.

It was during a kayaking trip to Chile in 2014 that Rok was inspired to save rivers. There he met Benny Webb, an Australian kayaker who was campaigning against plans to build five dams in the Marañón River, source of the mighty Amazon River, in Peru. Benny, in turn, had been inspired by a Slovenian woman, Anka Makovec, who had taken part in a protest in Tasmania in the early 1980s that helped to save the Franklin River. Rok planned to travel to Peru in 2015 to help Benny, but whilst researching that trip, he discovered that he was urgently needed much closer to home. The wild rivers of the Balkans were under threat from dams.

Hydroelectric dams use the power of moving water as a source of renewable energy. The water is collected in a reservoir and released in a controlled way to spin the blades of a turbine, which creates electricity. But they are not always as environmentally friendly as is often believed. To build a dam, a valley is flooded to create a reservoir, destroying the plants and animals that live there.

Families who have lived in the valley for generations

are forced to move from their villages, losing their homes, land and often their livelihoods. And the flooded areas actually contribute to climate change, as the drowned trees, grass and vegetation decompose and release the greenhouse gases methane and carbon dioxide. This is an especially big issue in tropical regions. Meanwhile, downstream of the dam, the dramatically varying water levels – high when the water is released and very low when it is held back – kill off fish and other river life, which in turn affects wildlife like birds and otters, as well as surrounding habitats. Smaller dams divert rivers into pipes, leaving long stretches of dry riverbed, with similarly damaging effects.

With its ancient forests, beautiful mountains, and wildlife such as bears, boars, wolves and lynx, the Balkans is seen as the wild heart of Europe. The continent's last wild rivers, still in a natural state and unchanged for thousands of years, flow through the region and much of the animal life within them can be found only here. The proposed dams would change all of that. Over 100 would be located in national parks, and all would have devastating effects on wildlife and people. Rok believed that the dams were unnecessary; the countries in which they would be built already produced enough energy for their own needs, so most of the electricity produced would be exported outside the Balkans. Rok felt that they were simply a way for greedy people to make money through huge and expensive construction projects.

While attending a rivers conference, Rok became frustrated with complaints from others there that they didn't have enough money or power to stop dams. He was sure they could join forces to do something fun, simple and cheap that would allow people to join in. Then suddenly he had the answer. Without stopping to think, he stood up and announced that he and his friends would paddle the affected rivers the following spring, to tell the world what was happening. They would call it the Balkan Rivers Tour.

From making his big announcement, Rok had five months to plan the expedition. He found five people to join his team, mapped out their journey and raised money for petrol for the vans that would take them from river to river. He gave talks and publicised the event to other kayakers, environmental activists and the media. Preparing for the trip was harder than training for the Olympics, when all he'd had to do was eat, row and sleep!

In April 2016, the kayakers began their tour. Rok and his friends would spend six weeks paddling on 23 threatened rivers in six countries – Slovenia, Croatia, Bosnia and Herzegovina, Montenegro, Macedonia and Albania. For a total of 39 days, they kayaked those rivers and visited villages along their way. Rok spoke to families whose homes and communities would be lost to the dams. Many had been protesting for years, but people were not listening. They warmly welcomed the kayakers and the TV, radio and newspaper reporters who were following their journey. Finally their stories were being heard.

The Balkans already has over 1,000 dams, built in the 1960s and 70s. Rok was able to see for himself the devastating impact of dams on people and the environment. On Mavrovo Lake reservoir near the Mavrovo Dam, Rok paddled through a half-submerged church that had once been the centre of the drowned village. Near the Mratinje Dam, he learned that when local people there were forced to move, they had been paid only five *dinars* for each square metre of their land – the price at that time of a packet of cigarettes.

As they travelled, Rok spoke to fishermen who explained that fish numbers were dropping because fish such as the *huchen*, or Danube salmon, would normally swim up the river to spawn but now get stuck beneath the dam wall, where there is no gravel for the females to lay their eggs. They also learned about the threat to creatures like the rare Balkan lynx.

The kayakers explored inacccssible canyons, adventured on wild white water and travelled down rivers of breathtaking beauty. But they also saw ugliness and destruction. They were stopped from visiting a dam construction site by road, so the next day they paddled to it instead, passing machinery and dredged riverbeds along the way. At one new dam, the manager pressed a button on his smartphone to release water into a canyon so that the kayakers could paddle down it. It was an amazing place, but they knew that all life in the river had already been destroyed and that, when they left, the riverbed would be dry once more.

During their trip, Rok and his friends were joined by 500 kayakers and 1,500 activists from 18 countries. Some joined for days, some for weeks. They organised protests, bringing together villagers and scientists, fishermen and farmers. They always made time to hang out with new friends, play football with the village kids, or enjoy a drink with the locals. As they travelled, they shared their experiences and photos on social media, and their stories were reported on TV and in newspapers all over the world.

The last river the friends kayaked was the Vjosa,

which runs through Greece and Albania and is the longest free-flowing river in Europe. Here environmental groups and schoolchildren gathered on the riverbank to protest against a dam planned for nearby Poçem. The campaigners believed that, instead of being dammed to create hydroelectric power, the river should be turned into Europe's first Wild River National Park, which would bring visitors and jobs through sustainable tourism.

During the tour, Rok had collected signatures on his kayak as a petition in support of the Vjosa National Park. On the last day, the kayakers and hundreds of people gathered in Albania's capital city, Tirana. Rok gave a speech and then tried to deliver the kayak to the doorstep of the Prime Minister's office. But police stopped him, and the kayak, which had sped down some of the most beautiful rivers in Europe, was left in the road.

But despite this final obstacle, Rok's first Balkan Rivers Tour had been a huge success. It was the biggest ever river conservation protest in Europe and had raised awareness of the negative impacts of dams and the ongoing threat to the Balkans' rivers. It has so far helped to stop six dams from being built.

Rok has decided to dedicate his life to protecting

wild rivers. Together with his friends, he has formed a organisation called the Balkan River Defence, which works with local activists and scientists to fight for rivers and wildlife, but most importantly to give a voice to local people. They want to show that there are other ways to use rivers without destroying them; each year they gather kayakers from all over the world to protest against dams while camping, enjoying live music and local food, and paddling the beautiful wild water.

Rok believes passionately that you don't need to be a scientist to conserve nature, you just need to have a voice. For him, conservation is cool and only positivity can overcome negativity and greed. And as the adventures of this free-spirited and fun-loving activist prove, there's nothing better than doing good while doing something you love.

AMELIA TELFORD

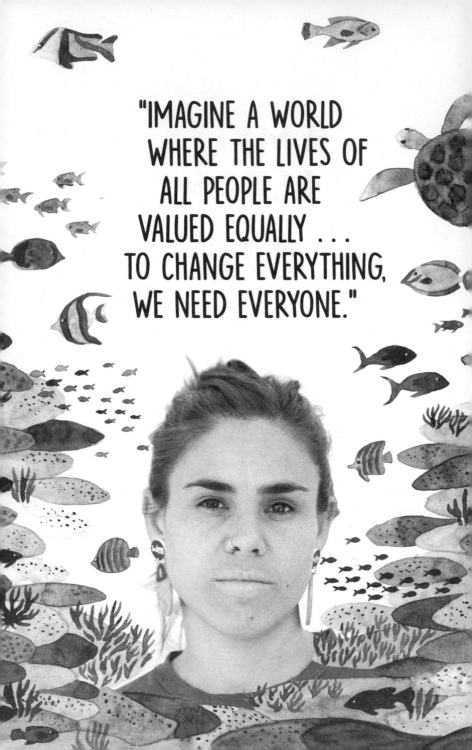

"IMAGINE A WORLD
WHERE THE LIVES OF
ALL PEOPLE ARE
VALUED EQUALLY . . .
TO CHANGE EVERYTHING,
WE NEED EVERYONE."

AMELIA TELFORD

CAMPAIGNER FOR CLIMATE JUSTICE

The Prime Minister got out of his car and posed in the sunshine, waving and smiling to photographers. There were cheers and jeers from the crowd on the pavement, some carrying placards. Amelia was excited and anxious. She'd been waiting for two hours and was hot inside her orange and white Nemo fish costume. In front of her she held a sign which demanded 'Reef not coal!' As the Prime Minister passed her, Amelia stepped towards him. "Prime Minister!" she shouted. "How are you going to protect my home, as a clown fish in the Great Barrier Reef?" He looked at her briefly, frowned and then carried on.

It was August 2013. Teenager Amelia Telford, known as Millie to her friends, was following then Prime Minister Kevin Rudd on his campaign trail before the Australian elections. Amelia is the leader of the charity SEED – Australia's Indigenous youth climate justice network. She and the other young people dressed up as characters from the animated film *Finding Nemo* were protesting against plans to enlarge a port on the coast of Queensland in north-eastern Australia to be used by the proposed Carmichael coal mine. The country is the world's biggest exporter of coal, which releases the most greenhouse gases of all fossil fuels. Dredging the coast to expand the port there could damage the nearby Great Barrier Reef – one of Australia's most precious ecosystems, or living environments. And greenhouse gases from burning the coal would cause the oceans to warm and become more acidic, which could eventually destroy the reef.

Climate change is affecting Australia in other ways too. The country is suffering rising sea levels, droughts and bushfires, and in recent years it has experienced some of its hottest temperatures on record. Summer heatwaves of almost 50 degrees Celsius have melted roads, seen thousands of dead spectacled fruit bats falling out of the trees and killed up to a million fish in the Murray–Darling basin. Indigenous Australians – the Aboriginal and Torres Strait Islander peoples – are particularly badly affected. Mining is threatening ancient Aboriginal lands while Torres Strait Islanders face the loss of their islands to the ocean, since many are less than a metre above sea level.

It was Amelia's Aboriginal roots that first led her to climate change activism. Amelia grew up on the coast of New South Wales with two brothers, spending lots of time outdoors exploring the beaches, mountains and bushland near her home. Her mother is from New Zealand and her father is from the Bundjalung nation and of South Sea Islander descent. While at high school, Amelia was learning about climate change when she noticed that the coast near her own home was affected by erosion – the land was being worn away by the sea. She felt a deep responsibility to protect the natural world, so she joined her school climate action group. Soon she was on the school environment committee and helped to get recycling introduced and solar panels installed at the school. She and her fellow students went on to write a 10-year plan, explaining how the school could move to 100 per cent renewable energy by 2023.

It was while learning about climate change that

Amelia became aware of its effects on Australia's Aboriginal and Torres Strait Islander peoples. Theirs is the oldest living culture on Earth. Aboriginal and Torres Strait Islander peoples feel that they belong to the land, rather than the land belonging to them and this influences how they take care of it. They have always lived sustainably, using natural resources with care. The desert, mountains, bush and sea – the individual rocks and trees – hold special meaning for them, and when the land is damaged or destroyed they are affected very deeply.

Aboriginal and Torres Strait Islander peoples had lived in Australia for around 50,000 years when Captain Cook landed in 1770 and claimed it as British territory. Britain began sending convicted criminals there in the late 1700s and seized land for farms and ranches. Over two centuries, the settlers killed many of the Indigenous peoples, and in later years children were taken away from their families and sent to new homes so that they would not be raised with their traditional culture and language. In 2008, the Australian Prime Minister apologised for these 'Stolen Generations' and today some ancestral lands are being returned to Aboriginal and Torres Strait Islander peoples as the government tries to correct some of the wrongs of the past. However, as a result of their suffering, many Aboriginal and Torres Strait Islander peoples today live in poor communities without access to the land of their ancestors and with fewer resources to deal with the effects of climate change, such as sea level rise, droughts and lack of clean drinking water.

Amelia felt that Indigenous peoples had important wisdom to share but were not always heard, so she was excited to be asked to give a speech at a national climate change rally organised by the Australian Youth Climate Coalition (AYCC). There she spoke powerfully on behalf of young Indigenous Australians about why climate change mattered to them. She had arranged for 60 students from her school to take part in the event, but while she was thrilled to see so many other young climate activists, she was disappointed that there were so few Indigenous campaigners among them. She spoke to the event organiser, Anna Rose, about her feelings and Anna invited her to become the AYCC coordinator for Indigenous youth.

In 2012, Amelia was thrilled to be selected to join the International Antarctic Expedition. She was one of a group of young people learning about the impact of climate change on one of the planet's most untouched and unspoiled areas and thinking about how they could make a positive difference to the world. Later that year, Amelia also had the opportunity to trek up Mount Everest in Nepal as part of AYCC's 'Climb-it for Climate' project. Here she marvelled at the breathtaking scenery, but also learned from her local guide how changing weather patterns and melting glaciers were having a terrible effect on the people of the Himalayas. Climate change was a problem for communities everywhere.

After finishing high school, Amelia decided to defer her place at university and work for the AYCC instead. She had wanted to study medicine because Indigenous peoples suffer more health problems than most Australians. But although she had worked hard to earn her university place, she felt that preventing climate change would have a greater overall impact on their wellbeing. Her father was unhappy with her decision, concerned that she was wasting educational opportunities that his generation hadn't had, but Amelia was determined.

In 2014, while working at AYCC, Amelia raised funds to launch SEED, a branch of AYCC led by Indigenous youth. Amelia was its national director. Over the last five years, the organisation has grown, with a network of over 200 volunteers across the country. Amelia has trained many young Aboriginal and Torres Strait Islander people to be confident in speaking out and organising their own climate change actions. Their aims are to fight fossil fuel mining in Australia, while highlighting the effects of climate change on Indigenous peoples. They see this as a matter of climate justice, arguing that although climate change affects everyone, the impact is not evenly distributed. Too often, the world's poorest and most vulnerable communities are hit first and hardest. SEED believes that the climate emergency is an opportunity to build a fairer world for everyone, powered by renewable energy.

Through SEED, Amelia has fought against the Carmichael mine, which will be among the world's largest. The mine threatens wildlife and Aboriginal and Torres Strait Islander ancestral land and culture, both directly in its construction and indirectly through contributing to global warming. SEED argues that the carbon emissions from burning coal from the new mine goes against global attempts to limit warming to less than two degrees Celsius, as set out in the 2015 Paris Agreement. Amelia and her team are angry that despite the fact that Australia signed up to the agreement, many of the country's political leaders support fossil fuel mining because it makes so much money for the country.

Adani, the company behind the coal mine project, needed to borrow money to allow it to go ahead. Always looking for fun and positive ways of getting attention, Amelia and her team organised protests outside bank headquarters, giving out roses to bank staff while asking them not to invest money in the mine. SEED worked with other environmental groups as part of the Stop Adani Climate Alliance, and Amelia and her team challenged politicians and business leaders on their support for the mine. Wanting to avoid the negative publicity of being associated with fossil fuels, several banks announced that they would not lend money for the project.

Meanwhile, in Australia's Northern Territory, SEED has campaigned against plans to extract gas trapped in shale rock layers beneath Aboriginal lands through a process called 'fracking'. This involves drilling into the rock layers to allow a mix of water, sand and chemicals to be forced through. This cracks the rocks and releases the gas, which is captured and piped away. The process can cause earth tremors and also pollute water. Most Australian states do not allow fracking, and SEED argues that the Northern Territory, one of the sunniest places in Australia, should switch to solar power rather than burning gas. The group has organised colourful, noisy actions all over the country to protest against fracking, including a sit-down protest in Parliament.

Unfortunately, both the Carmichael mine and the fracking project have been given approval by politicians. However, Amelia refuses to give up. She believes anything is possible if you are determined enough. She still hopes one day to study medicine, but in the meantime she will continue to lead SEED's fight against the fossil fuel industry and campaign for a move to more renewable energy instead, something most Australians support.

Amelia has described SEED's battle for climate justice as like climbing a mountain: they've come a long way, but they're still far from the top, and although they know their goal is possible it will take a whole team supporting each other to make it all the way. Above all, Amelia believes passionately in the importance of including all people in this fight, whatever their position in society or the colour of their skin. To find answers to the world's environmental problems we need to learn from people who have always lived sustainably from the land and have a special connection to it. Amelia is working tirelessly to ensure that those voices are heard.

ISABEL SOARES

"BEAUTIFUL
PEOPLE EAT
UGLY FRUIT."

ISABEL
SOARES

SAVING THE
PLANET ONE TOMATO
AT A TIME

Isabel and Mia drove down a dirt track between trees laden with fruit. They pulled up in front of a farmhouse, its white walls gleaming in the sunshine. Luis was already waiting for them with crates stacked up in the shade. The women got out and greeted him with a hug. Isabel picked up a pear from one of the crates. It was pinkish green and marked with brown spots. Next to the pears was a tray of tiny red apples. As Mia opened her purse and paid Luis, Isabel loaded the fruit into the back of the van. It was almost full of produce they'd collected that morning – knobbly carrots, skinny leeks, yellow-green spinach and funny-shaped tomatoes.

This was their last farm stop and soon they were driving back through the rolling countryside, past fields, vineyards and villages towards the noisy bustle of Lisbon.

Isabel Soares and her friend Mia Canelhas were in the Portuguese countryside buying produce to sell: fruit and vegetables that would otherwise be wasted simply because they were the wrong shape, size or colour. In the European Union, 30 per cent of food produced is thrown away because, despite its good quality and taste, it does not look as perfect as the supermarkets and their customers demand. This is part of a wider problem: it is estimated that rich countries together waste more than 1.3 billion tonnes of food a year. That is enough to feed the 820 billion people who face starvation worldwide.

Although it is possible to sell 'imperfect' produce to manufacturers of juice, jam and sauces, farmers don't always do this because they aren't paid enough money to cover the cost of harvesting it. Instead, this unwanted produce is sometimes fed to animals, but more often than not, it is simply left to rot on the ground. Not only has soil, energy and water been wasted in growing that food, but when it rots, it releases carbon dioxide into the atmosphere, adding to greenhouse gases.

Food waste also means wasted time for the farmers

who have worked hard to grow it, as well as the loss of much-needed income. Most farmers feel frustrated that customers are 'eating with their eyes', by always wanting fruit and vegetables to be big and perfect in appearance, regardless of flavour. In reality, the smaller, less attractive produce is often tastier.

Isabel was born in 1982 and grew up in a town on the outskirts of Lisbon, Portugal's capital city, where she lived with her parents and brother. She was an active child who loved playing out in the street with her friends but found it hard to sit still in class. Despite this, she loved maths and science and always got high grades. Isabel wanted to do something to make a better world, so she went to university to study to become an environmental engineer – someone who works to protect the environment by dealing with issues related to air, water, soil and waste.

After finishing her studies, Isabel got a job in Barcelona, Spain. It was here in 2012 that she saw a TV programme one day about the problem of food waste worldwide. At home that Christmas, she asked her uncle, who was a farmer, whether this affected his farm. She was shocked when he told her that he had thrown away 40 per cent of his crop of pears that year because they were considered too small by the supermarkets and according to European government guidelines. Isabel was outraged. She thought the rules were stupid. What if she had been a fruit? Then she would have been thrown away because she was short!

Isabel returned to her job in Barcelona thinking about what her uncle had said. Surely there were people like her who chose their food by taste and not by looks? Then she had an idea. She would find a way of bringing the unwanted fruit and vegetables directly to the people who would really appreciate them. She decided to start a business to sell the produce and call it *Fruta Feia* – 'Ugly Fruit' – so that people knew straight away what she was trying to do.

It was soon afterwards that she saw an advert for a competition to find ideas that would benefit Portugal. The winners would be given money to help make their idea a reality. Isabel filled out the form and sent in her proposal for Fruta Feia. In June 2013, she was stunned when she won second prize and 15,000€. That September, she gave up her job and moved back to Lisbon, feeling nervous and excited, ready to work on her new project.

Along with two friends, Isabel set up Fruta Feia. The prize money wasn't quite enough to cover their costs, which included creating a website, hiring a member of staff and buying a van to transport the produce from farms to the city, so they decided to 'crowdfund' the rest using social media. One hundred and seventy-six people gave small sums of money, and soon they had 5,000€ – enough to buy a big, bright yellow van with the Fruta Feia logo on the side. Then they travelled to visit farmers to ask if they would sell their imperfect produce. Isabel was surprised to find that many farmers were suspicious. Who would want to buy produce that they normally threw away? One even yelled at her, saying that for 40 years he had been told his greens had to be perfect, and now she was asking for the ones with marks on? They thought Isabel and her friends were really government inspectors coming to check their farms. It was a challenge, but eventually Isabel persuaded 10 farmers to sell their unwanted produce to Fruta Feia.

Next they needed customers. The team emailed friends, family and supporters, asking them, "Who eats ugly fruit?" hoping to find the 40 people they needed to start the scheme. Isabel was amazed and delighted when a total of 100 people signed up to be Fruta Feia customers in just one week. Each agreed to pay 5€ to join the club and to buy a weekly box of ugly fruit and vegetables. At the start of each week, Isabel and her team drove to the countryside to buy 'ugly' produce, which they brought back to Lisbon. They were given the use of a community centre, free of charge, and every Tuesday afternoon, volunteers met there to fill boxes with all the produce. The volunteers were mainly students and retired people who wanted to support the project against food waste, and in return they were given a box of fruit and vegetables to take home. Then in the evening customers came to collect their boxes. The scheme launched in November 2013 and immediately became a huge success.

Customers came from all backgrounds and their ages ranged from 18 to 80. When they arrived to collect their box from the centre each week, they felt like part of a big family and were happy to see the same friendly faces there. Many loved the fact that the fresh food had come straight to them from local farms. They also enjoyed the surprise of seeing what nature and the farmers had provided for them that week. And best of all, they could eat delicious fruit and vegetables, and save them from going to waste. Soon Isabel had a long list of people waiting to join the scheme. The farmers were delighted too, and it wasn't long before others were contacting Isabel, offering to sell their produce. Isabel loved the fact that she knew all the farmers and customers personally and she enjoyed visiting the farms to collect the produce and helping to pack the boxes herself.

As the story of Fruta Feia spread, they started to get lots of attention from newspapers and magazines all over the world, but Isabel didn't truly appreciate how important Fruta Feia was to her community until disaster struck. One morning on the way to the countryside the van's engine caught fire and within minutes the team had lost their only form of transport. Although unhurt, Isabel and her friends were in despair. How would they be able to get the produce from the farmers back to the city? But Isabel thought quickly. She phoned a restaurant friend, who lent them his van. When they finally arrived back in Lisbon, the team were three hours late and had only 45 minutes to prepare all the boxes – a task that usually took three hours. But Isabel arrived at the centre to find extra volunteers waiting there. They had heard about the fire and come to help. Miraculously, they managed to finish filling all the boxes before customers started arriving. Later, when customers, farmers and supporters learned what had happened, they rallied round to help buy a new van. Thanks to their amazing generosity, Fruta Feia would carry on.

The money Fruta Feia makes is used to help the scheme reach more people. Since starting, and with the help of some awards and a grant from the European Union, they have grown from 100 customers, 10 farmers and one delivery point in Lisbon to 5,500 customers, 213 farmers and 11 delivery points in seven Portuguese cities. Every week they stop 15 tonnes of fruit and vegetables from being thrown away. They also run workshops in schools to raise awareness about the impact of food waste. This includes a fruit challenge, where children taste both beautiful and ugly fruit while blindfolded and try to choose the beautiful one. Of course, they find it impossible to tell the difference.

Isabel loves her job because it combines problem-solving with spending time out in the countryside. She gets great satisfaction from helping farmers by buying their produce at a fair price and stopping it being thrown away. And she still finds it thrilling to see how her brilliant idea has become a reality.

Isabel plans to keep expanding her scheme across Portugal. Today, there are similar projects starting elsewhere in Europe and in the USA, and it seems that Fruta Feia is inspiring supermarkets to take action too. The first supermarket chain to sell imperfect produce was Intermarché in France. They named their range

Les Fruits et Légumes Moches – Ugly Fruit and Vegetables.

Perhaps one day supermarkets will sell *all* fruits and vegetables regardless of their shape, size or colour. Isabel hopes so and that Fruta Feia will no longer be needed. Until then she will carry on working for change, supported by the farmers and volunteers who love what she is doing. And, of course, none of this would be possible without her loyal customers – the beautiful people who eat ugly fruit.

WILLIAM KAMKWAMBA

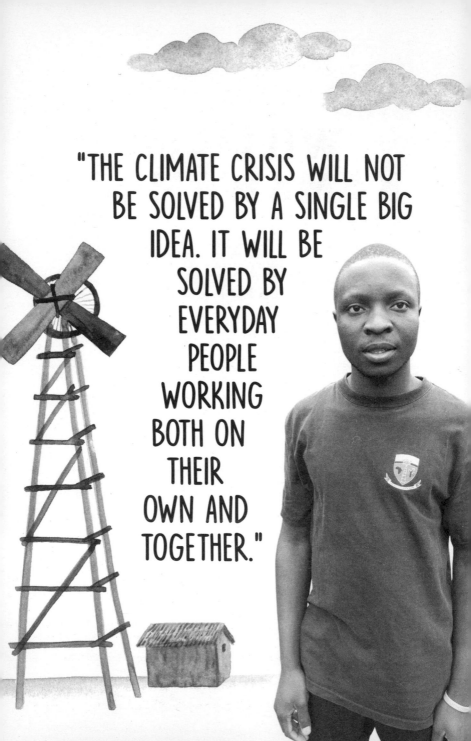

"THE CLIMATE CRISIS WILL NOT BE SOLVED BY A SINGLE BIG IDEA. IT WILL BE SOLVED BY EVERYDAY PEOPLE WORKING BOTH ON THEIR OWN AND TOGETHER."

WILLIAM KAMKWAMBA

THE BOY
WHO BUILT
WINDMILLS

William put down his hoe and wiped his brow. It was only 7 a.m. but he was already sweating beneath a cloudless sky and white sun. Blue gum trees shimmered in the heat. He looked at his morning's work – long ridges of dry, red earth ready for planting. His stomach gnawed with hunger. He had woken at 4 a.m. to come to the fields in the cool, but there hadn't been enough grain for him to have porridge. It was almost time for school. Perhaps this would take his mind off his empty stomach.

It was November 2001. Fourteen-year-old William Kamkwamba was helping his father in the fields.

William lived with his parents and six sisters in Masitala Village in Wimbe, Malawi. His father was a farmer who grew their food and a little tobacco to sell. Their last maize harvest had been very poor and they now only had five sacks left instead of the usual full grain store. The previous December's rains had arrived late and caused floods. Then the rains had stopped and the country had been hit by drought. This change in weather patterns was due to climate change and it had damaged the precious maize crop they relied on during the 'hungry season' – the period from October to February when nothing is harvested from the land. William wondered how they would survive until March, when the first maize would be ready to eat.

Life was tough in his village. William's mother spent an hour each day drawing water from the well, while his sisters could spend three hours collecting firewood from the forest. William wanted to study science so he could become an engineer and make life better for his family. Ever since he was small, he had always been curious about how things worked. He had taken apart his father's old radio and fixed it, and by the time he was 13 he was regularly repairing radios for neighbours. He knew he needed to do well in secondary school to achieve his aim, but his grades were disappointing. He wished they had electricity so he could study in the evenings.

By December, the family was eating just one meal a day, and William's only distraction from hunger was his excitement about starting secondary school in January. But when the time came, he was only able to attend for a single month, because his family could not afford to pay the fees. Across Malawi, the famine was getting worse. William saw the look of worry in his parents' eyes. They were forced to sell their goats and use the last of their savings to buy extra grain.

William missed school terribly. He would wait for his friend Gilbert each afternoon, eager to see his notes and hear what he had learned, until the school itself closed due to the famine. William became a regular visitor to the small community library. He always chose science books and was fascinated to learn about electricity. Many of the books were in English, so whenever he didn't understand the words, he asked the librarian to help him. Then one morning, he picked up an old textbook called *Using Energy*. It had a picture of wind turbines on the cover, and turning the pages, William read that these could be used to generate electricity and pump water from deep underground. In that moment, he had a dream. Now he knew how to provide light for his family and water so they could always grow food regardless of the rains: he would build a windmill.

By the end of March, the first young maize was ready to eat at last. William's family were grateful to have survived the famine, but many others weren't so lucky. It had been the worst in Malawi's history and many hundreds of people had died.

School reopened in May and William tried to sneak back into lessons, but he was eventually found out and asked to leave. William was unhappy, thinking he had no hope of becoming anything more than a poor farmer, so when he wasn't helping his father, he threw himself into his windmill project. Now the local junkyard became his favourite place. He saw treasure in the things that people threw away. He collected anything that might be useful – wooden poles, old pumps, broken pipes, worn-out shoes, copper wires, car batteries, his father's battered bicycle – and stored them in his bedroom. Children from school told him he was dirty for scrabbling around in the junk. His mum was horrified that he would hoard scrap in his room. His sisters hovered at his door, wanting to know what he was doing. William told them all to wait and see.

First, William tested his idea by making a small windmill with blades made from a cut and flattened plastic tub and an old radio motor as the generator. He was thrilled when he held it to the wind and the spinning blades generated electricity to power his radio. Now he would make a bigger one. He worked in secret, away from the house, but Gilbert, and William's cousin Geoffrey, often came to watch. When William couldn't find parts, he made them himself. He cut PVC pipes, heated them and pounded them into shape to create blades, and flattened beer bottle caps to use as washers. He planned to use the spinning blades to turn the back wheel of his dad's cut-down bike, but there were some things he still needed to buy to finish the windmill – nuts and bolts, and a bike dynamo to make the generator. He had no money to buy these things. It looked like he might have to abandon his dream. Fortunately Gilbert refused to let that happen. William's friend used the little money he had to buy everything William still needed. The project was back on.

The finished windmill was nearly three metres wide. Now William needed to raise it into the sky where it could catch the most wind. His friends helped him chop down some tall blue gum trees. They stripped off the branches and, with nails donated by Geoffrey, built a tower about five metres tall outside William's house, with branches nailed across its legs to make a ladder.

At last William was ready to fix the windmill to the top. William's family and a crowd of people from the village who had noticed the tower gathered below to watch.

With the help of his friends and a pulley and rope, William hauled his contraption to the top of the tower and fixed it securely in place. Then he carefully pulled away the old bike spoke he had used to jam the wheel to stop the blades spinning. The four blades turned slowly at first, then spun faster and faster as they caught the wind. William clung tightly to the wooden tower as it began to rock. He slowly pulled a lightbulb from his pocket. Holding his breath, he gently attached the wires from the windmill. William held out the bulb in his hand. There was a flicker … then another … then a bright, steady light. The crowd below cried out in amazement. William had made electricity from the wind!

News of William and his windmill spread quickly. Every day, dozens of people came to see it, with its bulb glowing bright. William's parents were so proud of their son.

Over the next four years, in between farming duties, William continued to extend his project. He rigged up wiring so that he had light in his bedroom; the switch was made from plastic piping, rubber from old flip-flops and some springs. Then he improved the design of his windmill so that it would turn faster and generate more electricity. Now he was able to power lights for the whole family home, as well as two radios. In the evenings, he, his parents and sisters could now read, sew and listen to their favourite programmes. William adapted a car battery so that they could store energy, and there was often a queue from their house to the road as people waited to charge their mobile phones.

William's parents still didn't have enough money to pay for him to go back to secondary school, but his old primary school teacher asked him if he would run a science club for the students there. William was keen to show children that they could make things too, so he built a small windmill in the schoolyard, which powered a radio. The children were amazed as William explained all about electricity. Then one day, when William was 19, an education official, Dr Hartford Mchazime, visited the school and spotted the windmill. He was surprised and impressed to learn that it had been built by an ex-student and went to meet William straight away. Dr Mchazime was able to help William return to school, and news of the boy and his windmill spread across Malawi.

As a result of the internet coverage, William was

invited to join a TED conference in Arusha, Tanzania, for young innovators. It was the first time he had flown in an aeroplane, something he could never even have imagined doing. At the conference, William was interviewed onstage about his windmill, and millions of people later watched the talk online. Thanks to this, he was able to raise enough money to build a second windmill and buy a pump to irrigate his family's vegetable garden. William's dream had finally come true. He had given his family security against hunger.

One of the TED conference organisers, Tom Rielly, was so moved by William's story that he offered to pay for his education for the next seven years. So after finishing secondary school William attended Johannesburg's African Leadership Academy, whose students are young future leaders from all over the continent. From there, he studied environmental studies at Dartmouth College, one of America's top universities.

Today, William works as an engineer, splitting his time between Malawi and California, and is invited to speak all over the world. He has paid for his sisters and cousin to go to school, and set up a charity called the Moving Windmills Project to support others in his community. Through this, he has helped to fund a new secondary school, as well as solar, wind and biogas projects and transport. His Moving Windmills Innovation Centre gives other young people the opportunity to become innovators too. Most recently he has created online teaching materials to help students in other developing countries find ways to solve problems for their communities.

With patience, skill and enormous determination, William has achieved incredible things. Inspired by a picture in a library book, one young boy's dreams have built not only windmills, but a better future for countless people all over the world.

DOUG
SMITH

DOUG SMITH

WOLVES AND WILDERNESS IN YELLOWSTONE PARK

Through his spotting scope, Doug watched the wolf pups at play. One was pouncing on a feather on the ground. A second joined in and soon the two were rolling in the grass. Nearby an adult wolf, lean and grey with a white muzzle, was trotting around with a long stick in its mouth, followed by four more pups. It was one of last year's pups that had stayed behind to 'babysit' while the rest of the pack was hunting. Then a large, handsome black wolf suddenly came into view. With its broad shoulders, grey-flecked fur and golden eyes, Doug recognised it immediately as Wolf 21 – the alpha male of the Druid Peak pack and one of the strongest yet gentlest wolves he'd ever known. At once, the pups stopped their games and crowded around their father, prodding his muzzle with their noses to ask for food.

It was summer 2003 and Doug Smith, Yellowstone Park Wolf Project leader, was watching some of the wolves that make the park world famous. But it hadn't always been this way. Until 200 years ago, wolves roamed freely in North America, but when European settlers arrived in the 1800s, ranchers and hunters killed wolves to stop them eating livestock and wildlife such as elk, which they wanted to hunt themselves. The park was created in 1872 to preserve the area's natural beauty; it is renowned for its volcanic springs, geysers and coloured pools. But by 1926 wolves had been wiped out from Yellowstone. The poisoning and trapping of wolves continued elsewhere until the early 1970s and wolves only survived in remote areas of North America: Minnesota, Western Canada and Alaska.

Without wolves to hunt them, Yellowstone's elk population rose rapidly. The elk overgrazed the grass and their browsing – or nibbling of young leaf buds – killed young trees. Park rangers now had to kill elk to control their numbers, and people began to ask if losing the wolves had been a good idea. In the 1960s and 70s, public attitudes to the environment and wildlife changed and in 1973 a new law was passed – the Endangered Species Act – to try to correct some of the mistakes of the past. Wolves were included in the list of endangered species that the US Fish and Wildlife Service was now legally required to bring back into America. Yellowstone was chosen as one of the places for this. It took over 10 years to get approval for the project, because so many hunters and ranchers objected, but it was finally given the go-ahead in 1994, when Doug joined the team.

Doug's love for wolves began when he was a boy. His father ran a kids' camp and Doug spent all his weekends and summer holidays there. He was the baby of his family – his sister, the next youngest, was six years older – so from an early age he played in the woods alone, exploring streams and lakes and watching birds. Aged 10, he read a magazine article about wolves, which sparked his life-long fascination with the animal. He set out to learn everything he could about them and discovered that they were the villain of countless children's stories. He puzzled over how humans could wipe out an entire animal species and dreamed of visiting the wild 'North' where the remaining wolves roamed free. When he was 12, his brother bought him a book about wolves and, aged 15, Doug wrote to the author and other wolf biologists asking for a holiday job helping with their work. But sadly no one offered him the opportunity. Still determined, he tried again at 18 and this time he got a volunteer position helping to raise wolf pups in Indiana. Doug went to university to study biology, spending his summers working with wolves on Isle Royale, an island national park in Lake Superior. When he finished his studies in 1994, he joined the Yellowstone Wolf Project, becoming project leader in 1997.

It was here, in 1995 – almost 60 years after the last native wolf had been killed – that 14 wolves captured in Canada were released, followed by 17 more the next year. It was Doug's job to lead the teams studying them. Their research allowed them to understand how wolves lived in packs, what they ate and to identify any health problems. This information helped the scientists to protect them, with the aim of increasing their numbers so that wolves would no longer be endangered in America. For their research, Doug's team fitted each wolf with a radio transmitter inside a collar so that it could be tracked as it moved around the park. At the same time they checked the wolf's health and took blood samples. To capture the wolf, the team approached it by helicopter and Doug fired a tranquiliser dart to send it to sleep, before being dropped off next to the animal. He always cherished those moments sitting alone with the sleeping wolf. Surrounded by the quiet beauty of nature, he would look into each wolf's eyes and imagine what its life was like.

The wolf population grew quickly before settling at around 100 animals in 10 packs, although the number changed depending on the amount of prey, such as elk and bison, available for them to feed on. Soon the elk numbers went down, as predicted, due not only to the presence of wolves, but also to cougars and bears. There was no risk of too many elks being killed, because the wolves only preyed on weak and vulnerable animals. Doug's team found that wolves lived only five to six years and could be killed by disease, wolves from other packs or even by the animals they were hunting.

After the wolves' reintroduction, there continued to be many people who objected to them being at Yellowstone. These people argued that the wolves would go outside the park and kill livestock, and that they were killing all the elk so that there were fewer for hunters. In reality, few wolves tried to leave the park, and when they did they were most at risk of being killed by humans. Doug was always sad to hear that wolves had died. In his view, the public don't know the truth about wolves and believe that they kill other animals for fun, which is untrue. People are also often surprised to learn that wolves are naturally afraid of humans. There are rare cases of wolves attacking people, but this happens when the animals have lost their fear of humans. For this reason, Yellowstone Park rangers have to kill wolves that have been fed by visitors. Since wolves were reintroduced, many people have used court cases to try to get them removed from Yellowstone. Although these have all been unsuccessful, fighting each case involves a lot of work and expense for the park's team. Getting enough funding for research has also always been difficult and the project relies on donations from wolf supporters.

Part of Doug's team's research was to study the effect of the wolves on the rest of the ecosystem – or all the living things, including plants and animals, interacting with each other in the park. While the team had expected elk numbers to fall, they were amazed by some of the other changes they discovered.

Firstly, the elk changed their feeding habits because of the wolves; they now constantly moved around to graze and browse instead of staying in one place. This, plus their reduced numbers, gave the land a chance to recover. When Doug first arrived, most willow and aspen trees had only come up to his knees and had been badly damaged. Now cottonwood, aspen and poplar trees grew again alongside the rivers, creating dense forests in previously bare valleys. With more trees came more berries and insects, so then songbirds and migrating birds returned. In the rivers, beavers, which had almost disappeared from Yellowstone, started to flourish. Beavers feed on trees and use them to build dams, which create deep pools where they fish in winter. Ducks, fish, muskrats, reptiles and amphibians came to live in these pools.

Other species had benefitted from the arrival of the wolves too. Coyote numbers went down because wolves competed with them for food, and as a result the mouse and rabbit populations grew. This, in turn, attracted weasels, badgers, foxes and hawks, who feed on them. Ravens, bald eagles and bears flourished because they are scavengers, eating the leftover carcasses of animals killed by wolves. The bears also had more berries to eat. Cougars and bears increased the impact of the wolves by also killing the elk and their calves.

But the most surprising thing of all was that the wolves' return had altered the flow of the rivers. In some places, the new trees stabilised the riverbanks with their roots, meaning the banks collapsed less, so those rivers became more fixed in their courses. In others, the beavers' dams slowed down the rivers so that they started to meander again instead of carving through the valley in straight lines. The wolves had changed the landscape itself.

Even after 25 years, Doug never tires of flying over the park and seeing its incredible wildlife and beauty. There are bears, elk, moose, bison, coyotes and cougars, and birds of all kinds, but it's the wolves that thousands of visitors a year flock to see. Their haunting howls can be heard through the park in the early morning and at dusk. Meanwhile, Doug continues to lead the project and regularly gives talks about the animals whose stories he has come to know. Researchers from around the world contact him for his knowledge and advice, sometimes because they are considering returning wolves to their own lands.

Reintroducing wolves to Yellowstone has taught scientists important lessons about the essential role an apex – or top – predator plays in creating balance in the natural world. Every plant and animal is a necessary part of a complex system of living relationships, and if wolves had not been reintroduced, today's Yellowstone would be a very different place.

Although wolves are no longer officially endangered at Yellowstone, Doug worries about the future of the park. As global warming changes its climate and plant life, wolves and other creatures won't be able to migrate to find food, as they might have done in the past. His hope for their future now lies with young people. Perhaps they can use the lessons of Yellowstone to build a world where humans see themselves not as top predator, but as just one part of nature's rich pattern. And in the meantime, he hopes that their childhoods might be blessed with wildlife and wilderness ... and stories of wolves.

MARINA
SILVA

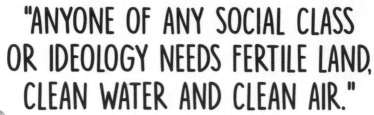

"ANYONE OF ANY SOCIAL CLASS OR IDEOLOGY NEEDS FERTILE LAND, CLEAN WATER AND CLEAN AIR."

MARINA SILVA

DEFENDER OF THE RAINFOREST

Workers brandishing chainsaws and sticks yelled angrily at the protesters. Undeterred, Marina linked arms with the people to each side of her and their group made a chain around the trees marked to be chopped down. She started to sing a Brazilian folk song and the others joined in, their voices rising above the rumbling of the bulldozers. Ahead of them, the forest clearing was an ugly sight, with bare, cracked earth and tree stumps. Huge logs lay all around – the remains of centuries-old trees. From behind them, birds and monkeys sounded alarm calls as smoke billowed into the sky, its smell sharp on the air. Another clearing was being burned.

The leader of the protestors, Chico Mendes, stepped forward and spoke to the loggers. After a heated discussion, they eventually turned and headed towards the road. Marina breathed a sigh of relief. For once, nobody had been hurt.

It was 1977 and 19-year-old student Marina Silva was taking part in an *empate*, meaning 'stand off' in Portuguese, a peaceful protest to protect the trees in the *seringal*, the rubber plantations of Brazil's Amazon rainforest. Brazil is the world's biggest exporter of beef, and ranchers had bought the rubber plantations and were driving the rubber tappers – the workers who collected the rubber – from their homes to make way for more ranches. Homeless families were forced to live in slums, or *favelas*, in the city. The rainforest was also home to Indigenous peoples – the original inhabitants of the land – and their forest areas were threatened too, although some of these tribes had never even met other humans.

As well as taking people's homes and livelihoods, deforestation in the Amazon has a huge environmental cost for the whole world. The Amazon rainforest – also known as Amazonia – is the largest remaining rainforest in the world, roughly half the size of Europe, and spanning several countries in South America. It is often called the lungs of the planet, as its trees absorb much of the carbon dioxide from the atmosphere, and without them climate change would be much more severe. It also helps to stabilise the climate, producing essential rainfall, while the Amazon River is the source of one-fifth of the world's fresh water. Amazonia is the largest and richest ecosystem in the world, containing millions of species of insects, plants and birds. Many of its plants are used to make important medicines.

Born in 1958, Marina grew up in Seringal Bagaço in a village called Breu Velho in the state of Acre. She was the second oldest of 11 children born to a poor family of rubber tappers. They lived in a wooden house raised on stilts to protect it from the daily rains. There were no schools. Boys usually worked with their fathers, while girls helped at home. However, most of the children in Marina's family were girls, so when she was nine, Marina became a rubber tapper, walking many miles each day to 'tap' trees to collect the rubber sap called latex. She knew her trees well and made careful cuts that were not too deep, to make sure they weren't harmed, before collecting the milky liquid in a container she carried on her back. At the end of the day, her father heated all the latex they had harvested, forming it into balls that his boss sold in the city.

Marina loved being in the rainforest. It felt so alive. The trees rose high into a dense, leafy canopy that shaded the forest floor. Creepers and flowers twisted around their trunks, and birds, from colourful macaws to tiny hummingbirds, flew among their branches, while monkeys swung overhead. The chorus of frogs, birds and insects was often deafening. Some days, she would hunt armadillos and *pacas*, a kind of rodent, or catch fish from the river. They were paid very little for the rubber they collected, so relied on the forest, the river and their vegetable garden for all their food.

Rubber tappers suffered many hardships. There were no doctors and their only medicines were plants from the forest. Travelling to the nearest city, Rio Branco, meant a long boat journey via the river, but when Marina was 12, a road was built through their area bringing new settlers – poor farmers who had been forced off their own land. The settlers brought new diseases that had a devastating effect on the isolated forest communities. Sadly, two of Marina's younger sisters died from malaria and measles, while she, too, suffered five attacks of malaria. When Marina was 15, her mother died of meningitis. Despite her grief, Marina had no choice but to work harder and help take care of her younger siblings. In those dark days, she dreamed of another life. She wanted to go to school and become a nun as she believed this would make her strong enough to cope with her suffering and sadness.

When Marina was 16, she became ill with hepatitis and had to go to Rio Branco for hospital treatment. While there, she stayed with relatives and, to her surprise, her father agreed to her remaining in the city after she had recovered. Marina got a job as a maid and also went to school for the first time, where she worked hard to cram four years of primary school education into one and became one of the first in her family to read and write. After this, she joined a convent in order to follow her dream of becoming a nun, and started high school. It was during that time that she met Chico Mendes, a rubber tapper who was fighting for communities in the *seringal*.

Through her friendship with Chico, she saw how the development of her region was damaging her beloved rainforest without helping the people who lived there, as well as being cut down for ranches and timber, the forest was being cleared for mining and growing soya to feed cattle, but this was only benefiting a few rich people. She was inspired by Chico's efforts and also by stories of great leaders, like Mahatma Gandhi. As a child, she would never have imagined that she, a poor rubber tapper's daughter, could become a student, but now that she had, she thought everyone should have the same opportunities. She no longer wanted to be a nun; she would use her education to improve the lives of the poor and fight for the rainforest.

Marina went on to study history at university, after which she got a job working with Chico. They set up a rubber tappers' union, to bring workers together to speak with one voice in negotiations with their employers. Inspired by the reserves where some of the Indigenous peoples of the rainforest lived, they had the idea that there should also be 'extractive reserves' – protected areas of forest for people who made their living by extracting rubber, nuts and medicinal plants from the rainforest. This would allow development of the rainforest in a sustainable way – it would not harm the environment or use up its resources. The reserves would also provide schools and health centres to benefit the people who lived there.

Together with Chico, Marina led and participated in dozens of *empates*, preventing the building of many ranches and helping to protect thousands of acres of rainforest and the livelihoods of hundreds of rubber-tapping families. Television crews from all over the world came to report on their story and, as a result, environmentalists joined the protests, putting Brazil's government under increased pressure to protect the country's rainforests. But it was dangerous to stand up to the rich landowners. Protesters were often beaten and sometimes killed. Chico himself had received many death threats.

Marina thought it was wrong that most of the country's politicians were from rich families and cared little about the poor, so she decided to stand as a local politician in order to speak up for them. In 1988, she was elected as a city councillor in Rio Branco. Tragically, at the end of that year, Chico was murdered by the son of a cattle rancher. He was the 90th rural activist killed that year. Marina and her fellow campaigners were heartbroken, but she vowed to continue Chico's work. Thanks to her efforts, in 1991 the first extractive reserve was created in the state of Acre, protecting nearly a million hectares of rainforest and managed by the families who lived there. It was named in Chico's memory.

In 1994, she was elected as a senator to represent her state in the national government – the first rubber tapper and youngest woman ever to do so. Here she continued her work to strengthen laws to protect the Amazon and encourage sustainable development. In

2003, she rose to the position of Environment Minister for Brazil and in this role, between 2004 and 2007, she worked to crack down on illegal logging. Large numbers of people were arrested, companies were closed down and equipment, buildings and illegal timber were seized. She made many powerful enemies, but during those years, deforestation of the Amazon was reduced by almost 60 per cent.

Despite these successes, Marina resigned from her role as Environment Minister in 2008 because she felt that her powers were being gradually taken away so that she was not able to make the changes she needed to protect the rainforest. Since then, she has continued as Brazil's most successful Green politician, standing for president three times and winning tens of millions of votes.

Marina has been recognised internationally for her work. In 1996, she won the Goldman Prize – the world's top environmental award – for fighting alongside Chico for the Amazon rainforest and setting up its first extractive reserves. Today, over 30 years after Chico's murder, there are now 76 reserves in the Brazilian Amazon, spanning over 14 million hectares. In 2007 she was chosen as a 'Champion of the Earth' by the United Nations Environment Programme, an award for outstanding leadership on environmental issues.

Marina's long battle to protect the Amazon rainforest is far from over. Brazil's new president, Jair Bolsonaro, is determined to reverse many of the environmental protections she put in place and wants to open up protected areas of rainforest to mining, dams and other development. This has contributed to a huge surge in deforestation and fires to clear the forest. But despite the challenges she and Brazil's environmentalists face, Marina is positive about the future. She thinks that they will eventually succeed because the fight for the rainforest is a fight for everyone, rich or poor. And however hard it might be, and however long it might take, one thing is certain: this courageous and principled woman has no intention of ever giving up.

YVON CHOUINARD

YVON CHOUINARD

THE BUSINESSMAN PUTTING PLANET BEFORE PROFITS

The shop was packed with people, shouting and jostling. Some held huge boxes over their heads. Others lunged towards stacks of televisions and laptops. As Yvon watched the chaos unfold on screen, a man and woman grabbed the same box, tugging and fighting over it. At the entrance, hundreds more people who had queued all night pushed their way in as security guards looked on helplessly.

Yvon switched off his television. The 73-year-old businessman opened his copy of the *New York Times*. He smiled. Good. There it was – a full-page advert of a Patagonia black fleece jacket and the headline:

"DON'T BUY THIS JACKET". The advert explained that it took 135 litres of water and produced over nine kilograms of carbon dioxide to make and transport the jacket. It concluded, "The environmental cost of everything we make is astonishing … Don't buy what you don't need."

It was Black Friday 2011 – the last Friday in November, when many shops and online retailers slash their prices and millions of bargain hunters begin their Christmas shopping. Patagonia is the hugely successful company Yvon Chouinard founded in the early 1970s. It makes outdoor clothing for climbing, surfing, skiing, fishing and trail-running. For many companies, Black Friday is the day they make the most money in all the year, but Yvon wants people to buy less even if it puts him out of business. This is because for Patagonia the planet is more important than profit.

Although his company is worth millions of dollars, Yvon doesn't live the life you might imagine. He drives an old car, wears clothes over 20 years old and, now in his eighties, still goes fly-fishing, kayaking, surfing and hiking. He prefers gardening to meetings. He never wanted to be a businessman; when he was growing up, his passions were rock climbing and the outdoors.

Yvon was born in Maine, USA, in 1938 and lived

there until he was eight, when his family moved to California. His family was French–Canadian and in Maine he had gone to a French-speaking school. He found life at his new school lonely and difficult at first because he couldn't speak English. Instead of playing football or baseball with the other children, he spent much of his time by himself, biking miles to the park or playing around ponds where he could fish and hunt for frogs, crayfish and rabbits.

In his teens, Yvon joined a falconry club to train hawks and falcons for hunting. He and his friends would abseil down rock faces so that they could look into the falcons' nests. One day they met some people climbing *up* the cliff instead of down. Yvon was excited by the idea of rock climbing and gave it a try. Soon he was hooked.

Aged 16, he headed off in an old Ford car he had rebuilt himself and spent the summer climbing. After leaving college, Yvon spent most of his time travelling and climbing and became an expert at the sport. But he began to feel unhappy with the pitons – metal spikes that climbers hammer into the rock to help them climb – because they had to be left behind, littering the rock face. Yvon borrowed money from his parents to buy an old forge and anvil, set himself up in the old chicken coop behind his parents' house and taught himself to become a blacksmith so he could make pitons that could be removed. In between climbing and surfing trips, he supported himself by selling pitons and other climbing tools that he'd made. He didn't have much money. In fact, he was so poor that on one trip to the Rocky Mountains he ate dented tins of cat food he'd bought cheaply, along with porridge, squirrels and porcupines.

But his pitons became very popular, and Yvon was able to hire some friends to work with him. By the time he was 30, his business – Chouinard Climbing Equipment – had grown to be the biggest climbing gear company in America. Throughout this time, he continued climbing in mountain ranges all over the world, while his team looked after his business.

During the late 1960s, there was not much choice in outdoor clothes. Typical climbing gear was cut-off brown chinos and a white shirt. On a trip to the UK, Yvon bought a rugby shirt to wear climbing; its tough collar stopped the ropes from digging into his neck. So many of his friends back home wanted one that he ordered lots more shirts, and soon Yvon's company was selling these and also making other outdoor clothes: waterproof jackets, hard-wearing shorts and gloves and mittens. Their first fleece tops were made out of blue material usually used for toilet seat covers. By 1972, Yvon's team were selling more clothing than climbing equipment so he set up a separate clothing company, naming it Patagonia after his favourite mountain range in Chile.

Through the 1970s and 80s, Patagonia grew to be a very successful company. Yvon had always seen himself as a climber, surfer, skier, kayaker and blacksmith who just happened to make things people wanted to buy, but now he realised he was a businessman, too, and this made him uncomfortable. He had always wanted to do what was right. When he saw that his company's pitons were actually damaging the rock faces he and others loved to climb, he decided that they would stop producing them, even though they were by far its most successful product. Yvon had always tried to ensure his business was environmentally friendly, but deep down he believed that most businesses were the enemy of nature, using up the Earth's resources and poisoning the planet with pollution.

On his travels, he had seen what was happening around the world: deforestation and melting glaciers, the disappearance of wildlife. The streams he fished in weren't as healthy as they used to be. Yvon read about global warming, the cutting and burning of tropical forests and the destruction of rivers due to dams. Yet, at the same time, he knew that businesses *could* make people's lives better; they could produce food, create jobs and cure disease. So, in 1991, he made a decision: Patagonia's mission would be doing good for the planet.

The caring approach starts within the company itself, and today Patagonia is one of the most popular employers in America. Their head office is run by people who love the outdoors. Employees dress however they want – even going barefoot – and can leave any time to go surfing, as long as they get their work done. Everyone eats together in the staff restaurant, which serves mostly vegetarian food. There is an on-site children's day care centre, which is unusual in America. This was started by Yvon's wife, Malinda, who also joined the company, so she and other staff could bring their children to work and spend time with them during the day. Yvon and Malinda's son and daughter, Fletcher and Claire, now work in the company.

Patagonia does all it can to ensure that its clothing is as sustainable as possible. Twenty years ago, it switched to organic cotton to cut use of pesticides, and the company ensures that its factories do not pollute the environment or treat workers badly. Patagonia only uses down – or fine feathers – recycled from cushions, bedding and clothes that can't be re-sold, and its fleece clothing is made from recycled plastic bottles. Other big companies, such as Walmart, have come to them for advice about how to make their own businesses greener.

Yvon believes that to save the natural world customers need to stop demanding cheap and disposable things, and urges people to buy only what they need and to make those items last. You can send your Patagonia clothes back to be repaired, or watch their online videos to learn how to fix things yourself. You can also return your old Patagonia clothing and they will find it a new home, and if it is beyond repair, they will recycle it. They never want the things they make to end up in landfill or an incinerator.

Patagonia supports good causes too. In the early 1970s, it helped a scientist to protect his local river from development by giving him office space and money to continue his work. Since 1985, the company has donated millions of dollars to thousands of small organisations working for the environment. They do this through their scheme '1% for the Planet', where they give away one per cent of their annual sales to help projects ranging from creating an organic seed bank in France to stopping a nuclear power station being built in Japan, and from saving red squirrels in Ireland to protecting wetlands and native fish in Kenya. Thousands of companies across the world have followed Patagonia's example by introducing an 'Earth tax' on their own profits. On Black Friday 2016 Patagonia donated all its profits from the day – naming it '100% for the Planet'.

Over the years, the company has campaigned on many environmental issues, such as fighting truck pollution in the Alps and protecting the last wild rivers in Europe. The company is currently suing President Trump for allowing protected wild land in America to be sold to coal, gas and mining companies.

Recently Yvon has turned his attention to agriculture. Modern food production has a major impact on the environment. Close to 30 per cent of the world's habitable, or useable, land and 70 per cent of its water is used for animal pasture and farming. And due to modern agriculture's use of pesticides, biodiversity – or variety in animal and plant life – has plummeted. Patagonia has started a food business called Patagonia Provisions to lead the way in new farming methods that care for the soil, reduce pollution and which could even reverse climate change if they were introduced worldwide.

Today, Patagonia is still a family-run business, but Yvon is less involved and spends most of his time pursuing his hobbies. His old blacksmith's workshop can be found at the company's headquarters and he likes to go there to practise his old skills sometimes. He often gives his designers ideas for new products, like a surfer's cap he dreamed up recently while out on the waves.

Yvon loves to spend time with his grandchildren or on the river teaching young people how to fish. He believes it's crucial for children to grow up with nature in their lives. Because we protect what we love, and if we love nature then we'll work to protect it – just as he has spent a lifetime trying to do.

ISATOU
CEESAY

ISATOU CEESAY

THE WOMAN TURNING WASTE INTO WEALTH

Isatou stood at the edge of the village and looked at the ugly heap of rubbish piled high on the red earth. Amongst the discarded tins, food and bike tyres, one thing stood out: there were plastic bags everywhere. Mosquitoes swarmed above murky puddles of water pooled on bags on the ground. Two of her neighbour's goats perched on the rubbish, foraging for food. She shooed them away. Isatou had heard that many people's goats had died recently. When the butcher cut them open, he had found plastic knotted in their stomachs.

It was 1997, and 25-year-old Isatou Ceesay was taking a walk through her village of N'jau in the centre of the Gambia – the smallest country in Africa. As she turned down the dusty main street, women greeted her from their courtyards as they prepared vegetables and washed clothes. The smell of familiar dishes filled the air. Children played in a clearing by the forest, and cows grazed near a field of peanuts. Later that afternoon, she sat with five friends in the shade of a tree for the first meeting of her women's group.

Over recent years, Isatou's community had faced increasing problems with waste. In the Gambia, many people live in poverty. Here and in many countries around the world, there are no weekly rubbish collections to take away waste, so people have no choice but to leave it piled in the streets. Ever since she could remember, in her village, people had thrown their rubbish behind their homes. As a little girl, she had carried shopping back from the market in a basket, but then everyone started using plastic bags instead. Now those bags were killing animals, there were malaria outbreaks from mosquitoes, and vegetables weren't growing because of rubbish in the soil. Worst of all, Isatou had watched her friends burning plastic as fuel for cooking, releasing toxic fumes that were harmful to people. The waste problem was huge, but Isatou was determined to do something about it.

Isatou grew up in N'jau with two sisters and a brother. Her parents were farmers. As a girl, Isatou used bits of waste, like scraps of cloth and wood, to make dolls and other toys. This made her popular with her friends because children in her village didn't have many things to play with. She was a bright girl who loved learning and always came near the top of her class. Sadly, Isatou's father died when she was just 10 years old and her mother was left to support the family alone. Isatou desperately wanted to go to high school, but her mother couldn't afford to send her. She needed Isatou to work to bring money into the home. This wasn't unusual; in the Gambia an estimated 75 per cent of children do not have access to a proper education.

So Isatou stayed in N'jau, taking jobs and making and selling things. But she didn't give up her passion for learning; she realised she would have to find her own way of getting the education that she had missed out on. When she was 20, she sold the cow she had inherited when her father died and used the money to attend Gambia Technical Training Institute in the capital city, Banjul, to train as a secretary. After returning home, she became a volunteer with the US Peace Corps, seeing this as a chance to get more training while helping her community. It was through the Peace Corps that Isatou learned about the possibilities of recycling waste, knowledge that would change her life and the lives of many in N'jau and beyond.

Isatou's sister had taught her how to crochet, and this gave her an idea for how to upcycle the plastic bags that were causing so many problems – changing them from waste into something valuable. She would turn them into purses that could be sold to make money. Isatou persuaded five friends to join her to form a new women's group, and together they collected bags from the rubbish pile, washed them and dried them out. Then, that first afternoon beneath the tree, they carefully cut each bag into a long continuous thread of plastic several centimetres wide – called 'plarn', or plastic yarn. With this, they started to crochet small purses for coins, using different coloured plarn to add pretty patterns. It took eight hours or more to make one purse and each used up around 10 plastic bags. The women were delighted with what they had made.

Some people laughed at Isatou and her friends, telling them they were 'dirty' for digging around in the rubbish. Some men told her that her plans couldn't work because she was a woman and too young to be a leader. But Isatou believed in what she was doing. She loved helping others and relished a challenge. In her family, everyone had always worked together to solve problems, and her mother had been a great inspiration to her. In the Gambia, many girls were unable to finish school because they were needed at home to help their mothers. Isatou wanted women to have the chance to learn skills and to earn money, even if they had not been given the chance to finish their education.

Some men did not like to see the women working beneath the tree. Women were expected to take care of their homes and families while the men went out to work, and these men were afraid that the women would learn to no longer obey their husbands. Isatou moved the meetings to her house, where she and her friends could gather at night to chat and crochet purses by candlelight. They worked secretly for months until they had enough purses. Then Isatou took these to a market in the city and managed to sell them all – the city women loved them because they were so unusual.

The women continued with their tiny business, now also making shoulder bags and cosmetic purses from plarn. Many of them were earning money for the first time, and they were able to use it to buy food to help their families through the 'hungry gap' – the three months in the year when there were few crops from their farmland. Their husbands noticed how their family's lives were improving and encouraged their wives in their purse-making. The women no longer worked in secret, and soon others joined them. Within a year, Isatou's community recycling project had grown to 50 women and she named it the N'jau Recycling and Income Generation Group (NRIGG).

Women in N'jau were now able to save some money, and Isatou helped them to open their own bank accounts. With their savings, many of the women could afford to support their families in ways that would have been impossible before. Their daughters could continue into secondary school and they could pay for medical treatment when they needed it. The women helped their community, too, each contributing some of their earnings to start a community garden to grow vegetables, and to help pay for orphans to go to school.

But Isatou wanted to find more ways to share her knowledge and help people in her village. In 2000, she got a job as a language and culture helper with the Peace Corps and, through this, she helped to secure funding to build a skills centre in N'jau, where the women could meet and work together. Here they could learn about the importance of caring for their environment and about the dangers of burning plastic. Isatou started to teach classes on subjects such as gardening, soap-making and tie-dying, and the women were able to sell many of the things they made. She had learned about nutrition and gave cooking demonstrations on how to prepare meals full of vitamins and minerals to keep their children healthy.

The women of the NRIGG continued to make their bags and purses and, in 2007, they even started to sell them to people in America, with the help of friends Isatou had made through her work. They also began to think of ideas for using other types of waste. They turned food waste into compost for their vegetable plots. They sold scrap metal, turned bike tyres into jewellery, and crafted colourful bags from old rice sacks. They made beads from paper and even learned how to turn truck tyres into armchairs and stools. They made skipping ropes and used leftover bits of plastic bag to stuff footballs, so that local children had toys to play with.

And there were other ways they could help the environment too. People usually burned charcoal for fuel, and this was made from trees cut down from the local forest. The women found a way to combine old coconut husks, mango leaves and dried grass to make briquettes. These burned just as well as charcoal, but were cheaper and saved trees. They started to sell these alongside their upcycled crafts.

Soon the women had run out of plastic bags and other useful waste in N'jau, so they started to collect these from neighbouring villages and shared their knowledge about plastic and upcycling with the people there. In 2009, Isatou got a job leading a women's project for the Swedish NGO, or non-profit organisation, Future in Our Hands. This gave her the opportunity to work with many more communities throughout the Gambia, while also continuing her own education by studying for a diploma in community development.

In 2012, Isatou won a Making a World of Difference Award from the International Alliance for Women. Two years later, NRIGG became the Women's Initiative Gambia, and today Isatou has trained over 11,000 people all over her country in the dangers of plastic and the opportunities for upcycling waste. But her work has had an even bigger impact as, in 2015, the Gambia's government banned the import and use of plastic bags.

When she first started making her purses, all those years ago, Isatou's aims had been to solve the problem of plastic waste and allow women to earn money to support their families. Now she dreams of seeing more women leaders in her country. Today there are five women on the N'jau village council, something Isatou would never have dreamed possible. And as a mother to three sons, she sees it as her duty to leave the world a better place for future generations. She wants all children to have the chance to go to school. If they are taught to care about the environment, she explains, then we'll be leaving the planet in good hands.

Isatou has travelled all around the world to share her story, but she's always happy to return home to N'jau. Today, her village is clean and tidy and you won't find plastic bags piled in the streets. But she still remembers the villagers' struggle with waste. Where others saw a problem, Isatou saw an opportunity – an opportunity to create a healthier environment, but above all an opportunity to change people's lives.

CHEWANG
NORPHEL

"MY MESSAGE TO THE WORLD IS ACT NOW. BEFORE IT'S TOO LATE."

CHEWANG NORPHEL

THE ICEMAN OF LADAKH

"Mr Norphel!" Chewang heard someone call his name. It was a smiling woman climbing up from the stream. On her back she was hauling a plastic barrel of water that she'd just filled. He recognised her from his previous visit. Since it was his last village stop of the day, Chewang agreed to join her for a cup of tea in her home. As they walked to her yellow mud-brick house, he looked out across the fields of the valley floor. They were brown and bare. It was May, and they should have been green with that year's crop of barley. Looking upwards, he saw what he had feared: here, just as in other places he'd visited, the blue-grey glacier above the village had retreated higher up the mountainside.

Inside, as she boiled water for yak butter tea, the woman explained that the stream from the melting glacier had arrived late again that year. Her husband was out irrigating the fields, but she feared it was too late and their crop would fail. Normally peaceful neighbours had been squabbling over water, so they had asked a monk to come and perform a *puja* – or prayer ritual – to bring water to the village. But perhaps Mr Norphel could do something to help?

It was 1987, and 52-year-old civil engineer Chewang Norphel was visiting some of the 120 scattered villages in Ladakh to check on his projects. In over 20 years working here, he'd helped build almost every school, bridge and road in the region. With his neat hair and warm smile, he was a familiar figure whom everyone loved to see. Recently he had heard about the same problem everywhere he went: water shortages.

Ladakh, meaning 'land of high passes' in Tibetan, is an isolated region of northern India. Lying between the Himalayan and Karakorum mountain ranges, at over 3,000 metres above sea level, it is one of the highest inhabited places on Earth. Colourful prayer flags flutter above monasteries and *gompa*, Buddhist temples, dot the bare valley floor overlooked by jagged mountains. While few people live here, many tourists visit each year to enjoy the rich culture and trek in the spectacular scenery.

The region is a high-altitude desert, and temperatures in winter can fall below minus 20 degrees Celsius. It is even drier than the Sahara because it lies in the rain shadow of the Himalayas, which means that when air reaches this side of the mountains it has already lost its rain. Ladakh gets as little as 103 millimetres of rain a year and farmers depend on the water from melting mountain glaciers to grow their crops.

Glaciers are slow-moving rivers of ice formed high in the mountains. Layers of snow build up over years and become compacted into ice until they are heavy enough to move gradually down the slopes. Each year in spring the lowest areas of the glaciers melt and run in streams to the valleys below. But global warming means that more of the ice is melting each year, so glaciers are shrinking up the mountainsides. Added to this, less snow is falling during the winter to renew them. Ice higher in the mountains melts later in the year as temperatures are cooler there, and for the farmers of Ladakh this meant that there was no water in March or April when they desperately needed it for their newly sown crops. The lack of fresh grass meant villagers were forced to send their goats and sheep into the mountains to graze, where they risked losing them to attacks by lynx and snow leopards. Many families had no choice but to leave the land that had been their home for generations. It broke Chewang's heart to see people suffering. He had a strong Buddhist faith and believed our time on Earth is precious and should not be wasted. He wanted to use *his* time to help others.

Chewang was born in 1935 and grew up in a farming family in Leh, Ladakh's biggest town. As a child he helped his parents at home and out in the fields after school. He loved maths and science, and would often scratch out sums in the dirt as he watched the goats. Chewang was inspired by his father's cousin, who had studied in London before becoming Ladakh's first engineer and building its airport and first roads. But Chewang was the youngest of three brothers and because his family could not afford to send them all to school he was expected to join a monastery rather than go to secondary school. Instead, aged 10, Chewang ran away to Srinagar, 400 kilometres away across the rugged mountain passes, so that he could finish his schooling. While there, he cooked and cleaned for the teachers to pay for his food and a place to stay. He went on to study engineering at university.

On completing his studies, Chewang returned to Leh and immediately got a job working for his father's cousin as a rural civil engineer. He worked on many government projects and, as water shortages began to take effect, he was asked to look into building concrete dams to store water. But Chewang realised that dams could be very damaging to the environment and were also expensive to build. He felt sure there must be a better solution to the problem and began to experiment with different ideas. Then one winter morning he had a bright idea …

There was a village water tap near his house that was left running throughout winter to stop the pipes freezing. Chewang noticed that, as water ran to join the stream, some froze in pools in the shade of a tree. The ice pools grew bigger by the day, but meanwhile the stream flowed freely without freezing over. In spring, the pools of ice gradually melted away. Chewang wondered if there was a way to slow down the mountain streams to create shallow pools where water could be frozen and stored in the winter and then melted in spring. What if he could make artificial glaciers?

Chewang was excited by this idea and began to sketch some designs. Streams would be gently slowed by a series of walls until the water froze, little by little, as an artificial glacier. Wide streams would form frozen waterfalls as they made their way down the mountainside, while narrow streams on steeper slopes would first be diverted along a channel to a gentler incline. He would try to build his glaciers in the shade of the mountain, and always make sure they were as close as possible to the village so the ice would melt early enough in spring to irrigate the precious crops.

When Chewang showed his idea to villagers and officials to ask for funding, they called him *pagal*, or crazy. The idea of artificial glaciers was just too strange for them to understand. But in 1987, undeterred, and with only a few people to help him, he built his first experimental glacier in a valley above the village of Phutskey. As soon as winter ended, Chewang hiked up the mountain to check on his work. As he approached the valley, he paused, hardly daring to look … then his face broke into a smile … then a grin. The valley was covered in a sheet of ice – his first artificial glacier! When the ice melted that spring, the villagers were so amazed and happy to have water that they later helped him build the walls and channels to make an even bigger glacier, to provide more water the following year.

In 1995, Chewang retired from his job, but he

was not satisfied with staying at home. The water shortages were being made worse in Leh by the increased number of tourists, who expected showers and flush toilets, which used up precious water from underground. Water was being trucked in to the city and the harvest had been so poor that there had been grain rationing. Chewang wanted to put his engineering skills to good use, so he took up a position as the head of a charity called the Leh Nutrition Project and threw himself into helping as many villages as he could by building artificial glaciers.

Over the next 20 years, Chewang built 14 more artificial glaciers in Ladakh. While he managed to get funding from the Indian government and not-for-profit organisations, the biggest challenge was often getting villagers to support his 'crazy' project. The glaciers had to be created differently depending on the landscape and available shade, and Chewang needed their local knowledge to plan each one. But even in his seventies he still liked to hike up and camp overnight in the mountains to get to know the area himself.

Once local people understood how artificial glaciers could help them, they were happy to get involved. Without easy access to machinery and equipment, work was mostly done by hand using labourers and volunteers. Sometimes the whole village would help, including grandparents, although it often meant carrying building materials on their backs through steep terrain and working with the ever-present danger of rockfalls.

Chewang has transformed thousands of lives in Ladakh. Over the last 30 years, people have watched their mountains change colour as glaciers vanished, leaving only bare rock. But today, thanks to his artificial glaciers, some villages grow two crops a year instead of one and harvests are larger, which means some produce can be sold. Potatoes and peas now grow well and these fetch more money than traditional barley. Once dry and desolate valleys are looking greener than ever, and villagers no longer have to send their animals into the mountains to graze. Perhaps most importantly, young people, tempted to move away to the cities, can consider staying in farming, keeping families together.

Chewang has earned the nickname the 'Iceman of Ladakh' and always feels great joy at seeing the impact he has made on people's lives. His work for communities has been recognised internationally with awards including the Jamnalal Bajaj Award for promoting the values of Gandhi, and the Padma Shri, the fourth highest public award in India.

He still dreams of building new artificial glaciers, although sadly there is not always enough money available to fund them. Now in his eighties, Chewang can often be found at home, spending time with his wife, meditating or gardening. He likes to experiment with new crops – like tomatoes, aubergines, apples and peppers – that might grow in the warming climate and help his fellow Ladakhis.

Artificial glaciers are not a long-term solution for Ladakh because the streams that build them are fed by winter snowfall and this is threatened by climate change. But people have survived in this harshest and most inhospitable of regions for centuries and the project is buying them time. The future of this mountain kingdom is uncertain, but for now, thanks to the dedication of one ingenious and resourceful man, these ancient communities can live and thrive in the land they call home.

ELLEN MacARTHUR

"IF WE COULD BUILD AN ECONOMY THAT WOULD USE THINGS RATHER THAN USE THEM UP, WE COULD BUILD A FUTURE THAT REALLY COULD WORK."

ELLEN MacARTHUR

FROM SAILOR TO SUSTAINABILITY CHAMPION

There was an eerie silence as Ellen wandered around the abandoned buildings. Beneath the craggy mountains and blue skies, everything here was rusty red – from the cranes, chains and barrels around the harbour, to the corrugated-iron rooftops. The skeleton of a ship lay on the shore. Behind the crumbling pier stood an old factory with towering tanks where whale oil had once been stored. It was hard to imagine this ghost town bustling with hundreds of workers unloading bus-sized whale carcasses off ships and on to the docks.

It was December 2005, and record-breaking sailor Ellen MacArthur was in Grytviken, an old whaling station on the remote island of South Georgia in the southern Atlantic Ocean. With no regular flights or ferries, the island and its neighbours, the South Sandwich Islands, are hard to reach. Today, no one lives on South Georgia, but in the early 1900s this far-flung place was the centre of the worldwide whaling industry, with 500 men and their families living and working here, mostly from Britain. Ellen had wanted to visit these islands since she'd first caught sight of them four years earlier during the round-the-world race which made her famous.

Ever since the age of four, when she first set foot on her Auntie Thea's boat, Ellen had been obsessed by sailing. She saved up her school lunch money by eating only beans and mash every day so she could buy her first dinghy. She played with this in the garden until a family friend let her keep it on his pond. In her teens, she sailed in her spare time and started to compete in races – and win. As well as sailing, she adored animals and wanted to become a vet. Unfortunately, while studying for her A levels she became ill with glandular fever, and her grades were not good enough for the course that she wanted to do. So after leaving school she decided to work in a boatyard and focus on sailing instead.

In 2001, Ellen made history when she came second in the Vendée Globe solo round-the-world race, aged just 24. The Vendée Globe has been described as the ultimate test in sailing, as competitors race the 28,000 miles without stopping, and without any help from others. Conditions can be very tough, with icy cold temperatures, huge waves and violent storms, and of the 138 sailors who have attempted the challenge, only 71 have reached the finishing line. Ellen was the youngest person ever to finish the event. But second place wasn't good enough for her and so, in 2005, she set sail again, this time racing only against the clock, and became the fastest person to sail around the world, completing the journey in 71 days and 14 hours.

Back on dry land, Ellen was looking for a new challenge when she was asked to help make a film about albatrosses on South Georgia. She jumped at the chance. During the Vendée Globe race, she had passed a lonely island in the Southern Ocean – Marion Island – and been surprised at how green and lush it was. She'd been followed by the giant sea birds for days afterwards and had loved seeing them flying behind her boat.

After her incredible ocean adventures, the trip to South Georgia was the first proper break Ellen had taken in many years. But the story she was there to tell was a sad one – the albatross is close to extinction due to huge numbers being caught and killed on the long fishing lines of industrial fishing boats. This, and the dismal sight of the empty whaling stations, got Ellen thinking about how mankind affects the natural world and about how we use and destroy the Earth's precious resources.

Hundreds of years ago, our oceans were full of whales. But then they became a resource for humans – something to be used, just like trees, minerals and petroleum today. In the nineteenth century, whale oil produced from blubber was used for lighting in streets and homes, while whalebone was used in making the corsets that were fashionable at that time. By the beginning of the twentieth century, virtually all the whales in the northern hemisphere had been killed, but Europe still used a lot of whale oil – now mostly for margarine and soap – so the whalers came down to the Southern Ocean. Over the next 60 years, hundreds of thousands of whales were processed on South Georgia, until the mid-1960s, when there were so few whales remaining that the industry shut down.

Seeing the abandoned whaling station reminded Ellen of how she'd managed her own resources while living for months on board her boat during races. She remembered how she had carefully planned exactly what she would take for the entire journey, from every meal she would eat to how much toilet paper she would use, taking the minimum amount of everything. During each trip, she would waste nothing, switching off lights and computer screens when she wasn't using them. Yet on land people gave no thought to what they used each day. Ellen suddenly saw that the Earth was like a boat travelling around the sun. The Earth's resources were limited, but still humans took whatever they wanted, not understanding that one day there would be none left to use.

Ellen was so concerned about what she'd discovered, she decided she had to do something about it as soon as she returned home. As a child, she had loved problem-solving and finding out how things work. Now she started to learn everything she could about sustainability – or how to use the Earth's resources without using them up – and thinking about how things might be done differently with the future of the planet in mind. She spoke to experts on how countries buy and sell to each other and to experts on renewable energy, such as wind and solar power; she studied sustainable homes, visited an organic farm and a factory where they made electric cars. The more she learned, the more Ellen saw that so much of the planet's resources are wasted, but that this needn't be true.

In the natural world, materials flow: the sun's energy and the soil's nutrients make plants grow; plants are eaten by animals, which are eaten by others; and when plants and animals die, they decompose and their nutrients return to the soil. So it goes on in a circular motion. But humans have a linear way of doing things: we take, we use and we throw away. When a new gadget becomes available, or a new clothing style comes into fashion, we buy the new and send the old to landfill. And with each new thing we are using up a little bit more of our planet's limited resources and often producing toxic waste. Ellen wondered whether humans could follow nature's example – could we all live in a circular economy where things are designed to be easily reused or recycled instead of being thrown away?

In 2008, Ellen's friend Francis Joyon beat her round-the-world sailing record by two weeks, and Ellen was asked many times whether she would try to reclaim her record. But although she had never been able to imagine a day when she would not compete in sailing competitions, now Ellen was surprised to realise that she had found something more important to her than sailing. Though the decision to stop racing was the hardest she had ever made, she needed to take on a new challenge. She would use her fame to make a real difference to the world.

In 2010, Ellen set up the Ellen MacArthur Foundation, which carries out important research into environmental problems and works with businesses, government and educators to understand the idea of a circular economy and help them change their damaging ways of working. Within two years, she found herself speaking to world leaders at the World Economic Forum. Since starting the foundation, her team has grown from Ellen and a couple of friends to over 100 staff.

In a circular economy we will do things differently. Items like phones, washing machines and televisions will be rented and their parts and materials will always be returned to the factory to be made into new things. Already there are websites where you can rent outfits to wear instead of buying them, which means the clothes are kept in use much longer. One day, perhaps no one will own a car any more, but simply pay to use one when they need it. And imagine if we could collect all food and human waste and convert it into fertiliser and fuel that we could use.

Ellen thinks that young people will play an important part in making these changes happen. In the early days of her foundation, she went to a conference where a group of 16-year-olds had blown her away with their presentation on sustainability. From that moment, she knew that the most important thing for her team to do was to teach young people about the circular economy and to ensure that the next generation has the skills to rethink, redesign and reshape the future.

Looking to the past gives Ellen hope. When her great-grandfather was born, there were only 25 cars in the world and no one had ever flown in an aeroplane. By the time he died, there were over 100,000 flights a day, and mobile phones and the internet had just come into use. This showed her that great change can happen very quickly. Because of this, Ellen believes passionately that the changes *she* is working towards will be possible in the lifetime of today's children. And perhaps one day they will look back on our current way of using resources as we now look back at the whaling industry.

Ellen believes that humans are good at taking on challenges, and that history shows we can achieve anything we set our minds to. Ellen has always set herself bigger challenges than most people, though changing the way we use the planet's precious resources must be the greatest she has ever faced. But, as with the sailing races that made her one of the world's best-known and most admired sportspeople, this battle is one she is determined to win.

BITTU
SAHGAL

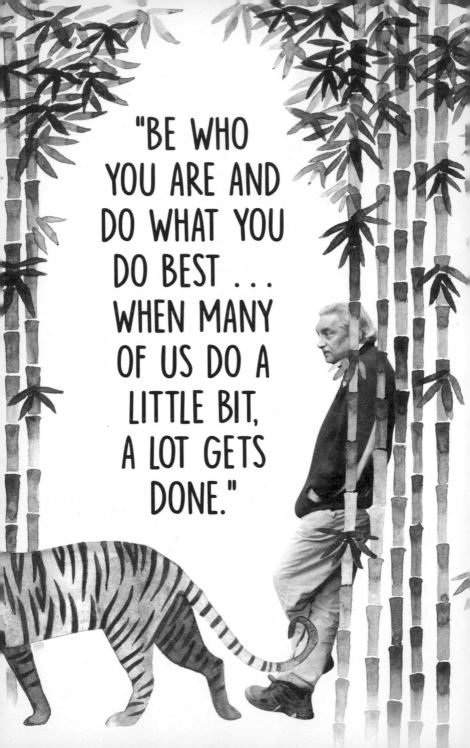

"BE WHO YOU ARE AND DO WHAT YOU DO BEST ... WHEN MANY OF US DO A LITTLE BIT, A LOT GETS DONE."

BITTU SAHGAL

SAVING TIGERS TO SAVE THE WORLD

On a hot, dusty street in Chandrapur, cars honked their horns while moped drivers and cyclists stopped and stared as hundreds of schoolchildren marched past. Chants of, "Save the tiger! Save the forest!" drowned out the noise of the traffic. The students carried placards in English and Hindi. Many had faces painted with orange and black stripes and some wore tiger T-shirts bearing the words 'Leave Me Alone'. The procession of 1,200 children poured through town beneath the bright midday sun. From the pavement, Bittu watched with pride.

It was December 2013 and the students were taking

part in a rally for the Kids for Tigers campaign founded by Bittu Sahgal, editor of India's longest-running running nature magazine, *Sanctuary Asia*. The tiger is endangered throughout the world and today most live in captivity in zoos. One hundred years ago, 100,000 tigers lived across 30 countries, but today there are only around 3,900 left in the wild, with 76 per cent of those living in India. For centuries the tiger has been an important part of Indian culture, art and stories. However, this magnificent animal is at risk as its forest habitat shrinks due to the rapid growth of the human population. This results in tigers straying into areas where humans live, where they may attack people or risk being killed. India has 50 tiger reserves, but even here they are threatened by poaching, illegally killed for their fur, bones and even their meat. Meanwhile, the country is experiencing the effects of climate change, with increased flooding, droughts and cyclones.

It was because of tigers that Bittu became a nature conservationist, or wildlife protector. He was born in 1947 in Shimla, in the south-west Himalayan mountains. His family moved regularly for his father's government job and although this meant Bittu changed school eight times, he also got to see many of India's varied and beautiful landscapes: mountains, deserts, jungle, grasslands, wetlands, forest and the coast. In his twenties, he moved to the city, where he worked as a salesman – selling everything from buckets and toothpaste to soft drinks – and later in advertising. But he never lost his love of nature, and continued to escape to the countryside whenever he could, often accompanied by his wife and two daughters.

In 1973, Bittu went on his first safari in Kanha National Park, one of the places that inspired Rudyard Kipling to write his famous stories in *The Jungle Book*. The park was home to leopards, foxes and jackals, boar and countless species of birds, but what excited Bittu most of all was his first sight of tigers wandering through the sal trees and thickets of bamboo – something he would never forget. Over the following years he experienced many other special wildlife moments too: watching blind river dolphins on the Brahmaputra with his young daughters, hearing elephants trumpet through a tropical storm and, in another reserve, watching a leopard and her cub cross in front of him just minutes after seeing a tigress and her two full-grown cubs in the same spot.

Bittu loved to travel, and as he did he noticed that wild places were changing as forests were cut down to make space for agriculture, roads, canals and factories.

There were new mines for coal, gas, oil and minerals. Hydroelectric dams and coal-fired power stations were being built to provide electricity. Bittu started to worry about the future of the natural world. It seemed to him that greedy businessmen were simply using up the country's resources without any thought for nature. At that time, Bittu was also becoming unhappy in his job and in 1980 he took a break at Ranthambore National Park run by his friend Fateh Singh Rathore.

One evening, as they sat by a crackling campfire under a banyan tree, Bittu asked Fateh what he could do to help protect wildlife. His friend's answer surprised him: he should start a nature magazine. There were countless Indian magazines about fashion, sport and politics, but not a single one about conservation. "If you teach people in the cities about wildlife," Fateh suggested, "then maybe they will do less damage to it."

That answer changed Bittu's life forever. With some savings and little experience, he pulled together a small team of skilled people and set up *Sanctuary Asia* – India's first nature magazine. Only 10 months after their conversation under the banyan tree, Bittu proudly took Fateh the first copy, which naturally featured a tiger on the cover.

The magazine had a shaky start and a few times

they nearly shut down due to lack of funds; Bittu was not from a wealthy family and he refused to borrow money from banks. However, the magazine grew more and more popular and many of the parents who read *Sanctuary Asia* asked for a nature magazine for their children. Bittu realised that children no longer had the contact with nature that he had enjoyed as a child, so, in 1984, he set up *Sanctuary Cub* which was soon taken up by almost all of India's school libraries.

Encouraged by the success of the magazines, Bittu began to look for new ways of spreading his message about the importance of nature. In the 1980s, he worked with a film company and some of Bollywood's best directors and actors to make 17 documentary films on tigers and a children's series about nature conservation. Millions of viewers tuned in to India's national television network to see the country's incredible wildlife and to learn the sad truth of how its natural world was disappearing.

Sanctuary Asia became one of the leading sources of information about conservation in India and Bittu was asked to join several government committees on the environment. At first he was excited at this opportunity to work together to protect nature, but he found that the government didn't listen to his advice. They went ahead with new projects such as roads, mines, canals and railways, which destroyed wildlife habitats, and also ignored his warnings on climate change. Bittu pointed out that there was no use building expensive dams below glaciers that would soon be gone if people didn't act, but he was regularly told that climate change was not real or that if people could live in the Sahara Desert, then an increase of a few degrees in temperature wouldn't affect the people of India.

Bittu knew that nature can heal itself and that wildlife will return if its habitat is restored. But he had grown tired of trying to stop adults destroying the planet. It was time to take a different approach. Bittu felt sure that, unlike their country's leaders, children understood the value of nature, as well as the threat of climate change. He believed that if every child was given the chance to fall in love with nature then they would grow up to fight for it.

Bittu decided to start with tigers. You cannot save the tiger without first saving its forest. When this is done, the whole ecosystem – every creature and plant in the forest – is saved too, even the insects on the tiger's back. The surviving forest soaks up the monsoon rains to fill up the water sources that feed India's wells, lakes, streams and rivers, providing water for millions of people. And those forests absorb carbon from the atmosphere, helping to stop climate change. So, just by protecting the home of one species, we could save *all* the natural world. Saving the tiger would be saving the planet.

So in 2000, Bittu launched his Kids for Tigers environmental education programme. His idea was to work directly with schools to give children in India's cities the chance to experience nature through film shows, nature walks, tiger rallies and festivals. Kids wrote to government officials to urge them to protect tigers and nature, and in the project's first year, 25,000 children and their parents took part in a tiger rally in Delhi. That year, they also collected over two million signatures and delivered them to the Prime Minister. After meeting with a group of these children in 2001, Prime Minister Vajpayee stood before India's National Board for Wildlife and asked, "Our children have woken up; why are we adults all asleep?" Government committees had ignored Bittu in the past, but now children were speaking out – and even the country's leaders were listening.

Today, Kids for Tigers involves a million children through 1,500 teachers in 750 schools across India. These children are part of a student army who happily march on the streets calling for tiger protection. When Bittu visits schools, he tells children that they are the voice of the future and urges them to tell the adults in their lives not to destroy their world. He thinks that it is grown-ups who need the most education and encourages children to explain to them the simple truths about conservation. Today, children who have grown up with the Kids for Tigers scheme have become committed conservationists and some are studying hard so they can find jobs protecting nature.

As well as Kids for Tigers, *Sanctuary Asia* also runs wildlife photography awards and a 'Mud on Boots' scheme, supporting people working in nature conservation. Now a grandfather to three grandsons, who are all happier out in the wild than in the city, Bittu still has no plans to retire. His wife and daughters tell him that he works too hard, but he loves his job so much that he goes to bed at night excited to see what the new day will bring.

Today, Bittu lives in Mumbai and while he often feels sad thinking of the forests, tigers, sharks, corals and species vanishing every day, he remembers to take joy from the nature around him. Even in the busy city he falls asleep to an orchestra of frogs and wakes early to birdsong, with peacocks and owlets visiting his courtyard.

Tiger numbers in India have risen from a low of 1,400 in 2004 to almost 3,000 today, and although the animal he loves is still at risk, Bittu remains hopeful about the future. If we can just slow down the damage done by his generation of adults until today's children are old enough to take over, he is confident we have a chance to put things right. Bittu has a motto: "Each one teach one." And as the children of India pass on all that he has taught them about working with nature, not against it, that is an important lesson for the whole world to learn.

———

SHEILA
WATT-CLOUTIER

"STORYTELLING IS GOING TO BE THE KEY WITH WHICH WE CAN CHANGE THE HEARTS — NOT JUST THE MINDS — OF PEOPLE."

SHEILA
WATT-CLOUTIER

INUIT ACTIVIST
FOR THE
ARCTIC

Sheila turned the pages of the magazine and looked at the photos one by one. In the first, a road was buckled like a rollercoaster track. Another showed a house tipping on its side, sinking into the ground. Finally, there was a forest with trees toppled in every direction. She couldn't believe these had been taken in her home region of Nunavik. But the Arctic was warming and the permafrost – soil that remains frozen even in summer – was melting, making once solid ground unstable. To Sheila, this was just one of the many alarming ways in which climate change was affecting her Arctic home.

Sheila Watt-Cloutier is an activist for the rights of Inuit – the Indigenous peoples of the Arctic regions of Canada, Alaska and Greenland. She was born in 1953 in the village of Kuujjuaq, Nunavik, Canada – a place of big skies, frozen oceans and endless snow. Winters were long and dark, with temperatures dropping to minus 20 degrees Celsius, and auroras dancing in the skies like shimmering curtains of green light. She lived with her mother, grandmother, sister and two brothers. The children loved playing outside, often sliding down hills on sealskins. Sometimes the boys built small igloos as playhouses. The family travelled by dogsled. Sheila remembers family days out, wrapped in blankets, speeding over ice and snow and through forests of black spruce, with her brother leading the dogs. The girls would ice fish on the frozen river while the boys hunted ptarmigan, a pigeon-like bird. Summers were short, warming to only 10 degrees Celsius. Then they would look for birds' nests and pick berries in the tundra, the vast treeless plains of their home. Sheila only spoke Inuktitut until she was six, when she started primary school. At home, her mother and grandmother often prepared traditional 'country food' of seal, caribou, whale or walrus given to them by hunters, along with berries and kelp, a type of seaweed.

Aged 10, Sheila's happy childhood ended when she and her sister were sent away to school further south in Nova Scotia, and later Manitoba. This was common for Inuit and other Indigenous children. Canada was colonised by the British in 1763, and many of the Indigenous peoples – those who had lived in the country before the British arrived – were driven from their land by the new settlers. From the 1870s, for over a century, many Indigenous children were forced to go to residential schools far away from their communities. The government wanted them to grow up in the *new* Canadian culture, rather than their own traditions and language.

Over eight years, Sheila went to three different schools, returning home only in the holidays. She often felt terribly homesick and missed her family. However, she gradually adapted to her new life and worked hard in school. Each time she came home, she was sad to realise that she had lost much of her Inuktitut language. Sheila wanted to become a doctor, to help her community, but her science and maths weren't good enough, so, aged 18, she finished school and returned to Kuujjuaq. She immersed herself in her native language again, relearning everything she had forgotten, and became a translator for doctors and patients in the hospital.

Over the next 20 years, while raising her own family, Sheila worked for both the health and education services, helping Inuit communities. Through her work, Sheila realised how badly Inuit had been affected by the loss of their traditional ways of life. They were now much more likely to suffer unemployment, mental health problems and to live in poor housing. Both the children who had been sent away to school and their parents had been deeply affected by the experience, and this hurt was passed from one generation to the next.

Then, in her early forties, angry about how Inuit were suffering, and realising she needed to find a way to bring about real change, she ran for election to a local organisation representing Inuit and became their corporate secretary. In the same year, she was invited to become president of the Canadian branch of the Inuit Circumpolar Council (ICC), an organisation which brings together representatives of Inuit from all the different countries in which they live. Sheila wasn't someone who naturally enjoyed being in the spotlight, but she was determined to speak up for her people.

In her ICC role, Sheila fought to ban the use of persistent organic pollutants (POPs). These chemicals are used in pesticides to protect crops and control diseases like malaria, but can also cause serious health problems. There is virtually no use for them in the Arctic, but in the 1980s scientists discovered very high levels of POPs in marine mammals and in the breast milk of Inuit women. Warm air currents had carried the chemicals to the Arctic, where they built up in the fat of animals which was then eaten by people. Over five years, Sheila worked to raise awareness of the human impacts of POPs and in 2001 helped secure an international agreement, called the Stockholm Convention, which banned their use.

In 2002, Sheila was elected International Chair of the ICC, a role in which she would fight her biggest battle yet: preserving her Inuit culture against climate change. The poles are warming faster than anywhere else on Earth. This is mainly due to the impact of ice loss on the albedo effect – the reflection of the sun's heat back into space. White snow and ice reflect a lot of light and heat, but melting ice uncovers darker land or ocean beneath, which reflects less light, causing more heating. Most people know about the effects of global warming on the Arctic's wildlife, but Sheila had seen its devastating impact on her peoples' way of life.

Long before scientists were talking about climate

change, Inuit elders had noticed their environment was changing. They said the weather was *uggianaqtug*, meaning it behaves unexpectedly. Once reliable cloud patterns could no longer be used to predict the weather safely. Hunting had always been an essential part of Inuit life and culture, but this was now much more difficult and dangerous. Hunters were sometimes killed or injured after falling through previously stable sea ice. In the past, they had built igloos as shelters while away hunting, but now the deep, dense snow they needed for this was hard to find. They had to carry tents, which were not as warm and offered little protection from polar bears. Increased rainfall and the early melting of ice caused dangerous flash floods as swollen rivers burst their banks.

Changes to wildlife affected Inuit too. Because caribou couldn't always cross flooded rivers, they were altering the migration patterns that hunters had relied on for decades. Animals that depended on the sea ice – like seals, polar bears and walruses – were less plentiful. And because of disappearing shore ice, polar bears were forced closer to human settlements, putting people in danger.

It wasn't only ice that was melting, but permafrost too – releasing greenhouse gases into the atmosphere and contributing further to global warming. Traditionally, Inuit hunters stored the meat they caught in deep holes in the permafrost, like natural freezers. But now, even a few metres below the ground, it was no longer cold enough to store their food. Thawing permafrost made roads and buildings unstable, while melting sea ice exposed coastal areas to erosion by the stronger waves of the open ocean. Entire communities were forced to move, as the land they had lived and hunted on for generations was lost or threatened.

With the loss of their hunting culture, Inuit were also at risk of losing the skills and values that their connection with nature had given them, such as courage, patience and strength under pressure. Many young people struggled to fit in to their changing world. Sheila wanted to do everything in her power to ensure her own grandchildren could be raised in the Inuit traditions that had shaped her own life. But she wanted to save her culture not just for her own people, but for the whole world. Inuit had lived sustainably from their environment for centuries. They had always understood that all nature – humans, plants, wildlife and climate – are tightly connected, and they had much wisdom to offer.

Sheila knew that time was running out. Inuit had

contributed little to greenhouse gases, but now their homes, traditions and culture were being lost due to the actions of people, thousands of miles away. In December 2005, along with 62 Inuit Hunters and Elders from across Alaska and Canada, she launched the world's first international legal action on climate change; a petition – or formal request – to the Inter-American Commission on Human Rights (IACHR). They argued that the United States was failing to reduce its greenhouse gas emissions and this was threatening Inuit human rights. This was the first time the Commission had considered a challenge from Indigenous peoples of one nation against the actions of another. The commission refused to hear the petition. However, Sheila was later invited to speak on behalf of Indigenous peoples at the IACHR's first hearing on climate change and human rights in March 2007. Here, as well as describing the impact of climate change on Inuit, she spoke passionately about its effects on other Indigenous peoples around the world, including rising sea levels submerging their lands and the loss of water supplies due to disappearing glaciers.

Although unsuccessful, Sheila's groundbreaking legal challenge did have an impact. Her speech led to a greater understanding of the effects of climate change on Indigenous peoples, and helped ensure that their needs and rights are considered when new international laws and agreements are created. In recognition of her efforts, Sheila was nominated for the Nobel Peace Prize in 2007 and has won many awards for her activism for Inuit peoples. Perhaps her greatest success has been to show the human face of climate change in the Arctic – it's not just about polar bears.

Sheila thinks Inuit are the world's environmental early warning system and that if we protect their home, we will protect the whole planet. She remains hopeful that humanity can come together and act before it's too late, by listening to the wisdom of people who have always lived in balance with nature.

Today, she lives near her daughter and grandsons, helping to raise them in her Inuit culture. And she continues to fight for their future. In 2008, the Canadian government made a formal apology for the way in which they had treated Indigenous children in the past. Today, the girl who almost lost her language is the loudest voice speaking up for Inuit peoples, telling their stories to touch hearts all over the world.

ANDREW TURTON AND PETE CEGLINSKI

"OUR MISSION STATEMENT IS SIMPLE: TO LIVE IN A WORLD WITHOUT THE NEED FOR SEABINS."

ANDREW TURTON AND PETE CEGLINSKI

SURFERS MAKING WAVES WITH THEIR BINS FOR THE SEA

Rows of yachts glinted in the sun as a speedboat chugged slowly out of the marina and towards the open sea. Andrew and Pete worked carefully on the edge of a pier. They were finally ready to test their new invention. Beneath them, litter floated on the oily water. Pete lowered their creation into the sea so it sat just below the surface, and fixed it to a stand, while Andrew plugged the cable into a power point. Then they held their breath as Pete switched it on. Slowly … slowly … a crisp packet and a plastic bottle started to bob gently towards the opening of the device … before being pulled over the edge and sucked inside. Success!

The friends high-fived and whooped with joy.

It was June 2016, and Pete Ceglinski and Andrew Turton were on the Spanish island of Majorca in the Mediterranean Sea, testing their first 'Seabin' – a rubbish bin designed to clean up litter from open water. Both were life-long ocean lovers having grown up on the coast of Australia. Andrew, whose nickname is Turtle, was a boat builder and especially loved sailing, often joined by his dog, Sam. Pete enjoyed all watersports, but his main passion in life was surfing. He had become a boat builder after giving up a career designing products such as kettles and toasters because he no longer wanted to make things that were thrown away rather than repaired. They met when they were working for different yacht racing teams, travelling around the world and visiting beautiful places. But over the years, both had noticed the ocean was becoming more and more polluted. Whether they were surfing amongst plastic bags off a tropical island or sailing into exotic ports full of litter, plastic was everywhere they went.

Ocean plastic pollution is a huge global issue. It's estimated that about 10 to 20 million tonnes is washed into our seas every year. Large quantities have collected forming the Great Pacific Garbage Patch – an area of plastic and rubbish twice the size of France, floating between the USA and Hawaii. It has even been found at the deepest point of the ocean, the Mariana Trench, 10 kilometres below the surface of the Pacific Ocean. It is a devastating problem, killing and harming marine life, and if the leakage of plastic into the environment is not stopped, by 2050 the ocean will contain more plastic than fish by weight. Much of this pollution is microplastic – tiny plastic fragments less than five millimetres in size, and plastic microfibres which come off clothing when we wash it. These are eaten by marine life and by humans in turn when we eat fish and shellfish.

As part of his job, Andrew had to clean the outsides of yachts, but this was difficult in marinas full of oily water and debris. One day in 2011, while working on a yacht in Los Angeles, he suddenly had a brainwave. If you can have rubbish bins on land, then why not have them in water? Over the months that followed, he tested his idea, using a plastic bin, glue, duct tape and a pump. His device worked, so he took it with him to marinas around the world. In 2013, after meeting Pete, he told him about his invention and asked if he could help turn it into something that could be sold.

Pete was excited and started thinking of how it

might work. Soon he had a design for a bin which sat just below the surface of the water, sucking water and floating rubbish into its opening. The rubbish would be collected in a 'catch bag', while the 'clean' water would be pumped out of the bottom. It would be powered by electricity and, just like a rubbish bin, emptied when full. They would start by making these for the calm waters of marinas, ports and harbours, where they often saw lots of litter. Pete and Andrew called their invention the Seabin.

By 2015, Pete had given up his job, to focus on developing the technology that would turn their idea into a reality. Meanwhile, Andrew decided to step back from the project to concentrate on boatbuilding, although he continued to help out. The pair had been working in Majorca, so Pete stayed on and converted an old warehouse into a workshop, buying machinery and tools to make the first Seabins – called prototypes – to test out his ideas.

While everyone agreed that cleaning up the oceans was hugely important, some people who had heard of the invention were worried that the Seabins might suck in and kill ocean life. To ensure this would not happen, Pete hired a marine biologist and surfer, Sergio, to help with the design, as well as two other office staff, Paola and Sascha, to help run the company.

First Pete shrank his design and made a mini-Seabin in plastic using a 3D printer. He added a mini-pump and installed the device in a fish tank for testing. Once they were sure this worked, the team made a full-sized version. To save money, Pete learned how to weld metal by watching videos and bought an old sewing machine to stitch his own catch bags from natural fibre. He kept improving the design, reducing the number of parts so that the Seabin could be produced easily in a factory. It felt like the perfect job, using his skills to create something that would help protect the ocean he loved. And living by the sea meant he could go surfing in his breaks. But by the end of that year the team had completely run out of money.

As they didn't want to accept funding from companies that were often contributing to the pollution problem, they decided to try to 'crowdfund' enough money to keep their Seabin dream alive by asking online for donations from people who liked their idea. They needed to raise $250,000. They made a video, and soon their sponsorship request 'went viral' – with thousands, then millions of viewers. Slowly, their fundraising total crept up. But less than a week before the end of the campaign, they were still $100,000 short. If they didn't hit their target, they wouldn't get any of the money that had been offered. Pete barely slept as he spent night and day contacting anyone who might possibly help. His hard work paid off. On the last day, they smashed their target, raising $267,000. They were proud that it was ordinary people – mums, dads and kids – who were giving them the chance to make the Seabin a reality.

There was much work to do to complete the working prototype, while also responding to hundreds of emails a day from people who had heard about the Seabin and wanted to buy one. But the hardest thing for barefoot, T-shirt-and-shorts-wearing surfer Pete was learning how to be a businessman. He often felt he was asking silly questions during meetings with companies who were interested in making their product, and sometimes even had to look things up on his phone to understand what they were saying. Happily, though, in March 2016, they struck a deal with a French company, Poralu Marine, to make the Seabins.

In June 2016, the first working Seabin was installed in Majorca. And over the following months the team travelled across Europe to set up Seabins in six 'pilot' locations. These were marinas and ports that wanted to be the first to have Seabins and had agreed to help test them. By November 2017, the testing was complete and the team were ready to sell their invention to a long waiting list of customers from all over the world.

Each device can collect up to 20 kilograms of waste a day, which means it can remove up to 90,000 plastic bags, or 37,500 disposable cups, or 16,500 plastic bottles from the water every year. Today, there are over 700 Seabins in 48 countries, each collecting on average three kilograms of waste a day. This is *a lot* of rubbish, especially when you consider that the most common items are lightweight – cigarette butts, small bits of plastic and food wrappers. In total, that's nearly two tonnes of waste collected each day from the sea. The strangest thing Pete has ever seen caught in a Seabin is a cowboy boot with a mini-pineapple inside. And once he found a $20 note!

While Seabins benefit everyone by helping to clean our oceans, they are expensive to make and cost around £3,500 each to buy. However, there are many communities joining together to pay for them. The port of Dublin, in Ireland, got its first Seabin in 2018 after 11-year-old Flossie Donnelly raised money by holding a disco, a quiz and a crowdfunding campaign. The Seabin team were so impressed with her efforts that they gave her two! In early 2019, 13-year-old surfer Archie Mandin raised nearly

$20,000 to pay for the first Seabins in the marinas near his home in Pittwater, Australia.

Pete continues to improve the Seabin design. As well as larger items, it can now filter out oil and microplastics more than two millimetres in size. He wants future Seabins to be able to trap microfibres too. The team hope that in future it will be possible to recycle the plastic their Seabins collect to make new Seabins, and they aim to have Seabins in the open ocean by 2027.

Pete and Andrew know that Seabins aren't the answer to the ocean plastic problem. The real solution is education. For this reason, they put half the money that they make into a charity called the Seabin Foundation, which teaches children about reducing plastic use, recycling and using science, technology and maths to invent new things to tackle environmental problems. They feel positive about the future because they see signs of change: shoppers refusing plastic bags, people carrying reusable coffee cups and children teaching their parents about the dangers of plastic to ocean life.

With a new baby son, Pete is more determined than ever to leave the oceans cleaner for future generations. Meanwhile, Andrew's niece Portsea Turton, who is studying marine science at college, is also a Youth Ambassador for Seabins and a member of the World

Oceans Day Youth Advisory Council. With the future in the hands of young people like her, perhaps Andrew and Pete will one day see their dream come true: a world where the ocean is free of plastic and we no longer need Seabins. Then they will happily get back to surfing and sailing the oceans instead of cleaning them.

RENEE
KING-SONNEN

"I AM THE CHANGE I WANT TO SEE IN THE WORLD."

RENEE KING-SONNEN

THE ROWDY GIRL WITH A VEGAN HEART

Renee was frightened, cold and exhausted as she pushed the last of the panicky horses into the trailer. Her waterproofs couldn't keep out the torrential rain. Tommy, her husband, struggled to shut the trailer door as gale-force winds whipped it from his hands. The farm track was becoming submerged under huge puddles. In the distance, green fields were now brown water as the flooded river Brazos crept towards their ranch. Over the last 24 hours, they had evacuated most of their 96 animals to a friend's ranch three hours away, but there were still three horses, three hogs and 20 cows waiting to be rescued.

It was September 2017. Renee King-Sonnen and her husband were evacuating Rowdy Girl Sanctuary – their farm animal sanctuary in Angleton, Texas, in the USA. Hurricane Harvey, a Category 4 hurricane, had brought a deluge of rain. They drove along flooded roads, anxious to deliver the animals to safety at the local showground before returning with a larger borrowed trailer to rescue the rest. A few hours later, their ranch and buildings had been engulfed by the flood.

Hurricane Harvey was the wettest tropical cyclone on record in the United States. Renee and Tommy were allowed to return home a week later, but they had to travel by canoe since the floodwaters were still high. They paddled through their barns, around islands of trees and peered into their home, full of filthy water. This was the second time in two years that they had been affected by flooding, although storms this big and destructive used to be rare. To Renee, it was a sign that climate change is affecting her country *now*. It made her even more convinced that an urgent shift towards vegetarianism or veganism is needed to help stop global warming. Vegans choose not to eat or use animal products, including meat, fish, milk, eggs, honey and wool. Cattle farming is a significant cause of greenhouse gas emissions in two ways: because of methane produced by cows and their dung, and also because land used for grazing and growing their feed is often cleared forest, which releases carbon that had been stored in the trees.

A vegan farm animal sanctuary is something you might not expect to find in Texas, home to vast cattle ranches, rodeos, barbecues and livestock shows. Raising animals – especially cattle – for food is a big way of life in this part of America. And Renee and her husband are two of the unlikeliest vegans you could ever meet. Ten years earlier, Renee had been a city girl who enjoyed burgers, shopping malls and yoga classes. She had been a singer in a band called Renee King & Wildcard and owned an impressive collection of leather cowboy boots that she liked to wear onstage. Tommy was from a family that had owned and run cattle ranches for four generations. After working for over 30 years in the chemical industry, Tommy had bought the 100-acre ranch to farm cattle in his retirement and when they got married, Renee agreed to move there with him.

At first, Renee had little interest in the ranch and Tommy's farming work. She stayed inside, keeping up her yoga practice and ignoring the cows that grazed peacefully in the pasture. Then Tommy asked her to bottle-feed two motherless calves, hoping to get her interested in ranching. This didn't work out quite as he'd planned.

One of the calves was calm and sedate. But the other was lively and fun. She was black with a white heart shape on her head, and Renee named her Rowdy Girl. Renee had always been an animal lover as a child – with dogs, cats and even a pet ferret. The more time Renee spent with the calves, the more she loved them. Soon she was spending lots of time with *all* the cows. She practised her yoga out in the pasture, where she talked to the cows, danced around them and even sang to them while strumming her guitar! She often liked to sit quietly beneath a tree and wait for the cows to come to her. Some would lie down next to her, resting their heads in her lap. Renee gave each of the cows names. Watching them, she discovered that they had different personalities and saw the strong bonds between the mothers and their calves. Then she learned about the red trailer.

At the ranch, when the calves were six to eight months old, they were taken to auction, where they were sold to ranchers who would raise them for beef. Renee couldn't bear to watch Tommy load up his red trailer with the calves. As he drove away, she saw the mother cows running alongside the fence, chasing after them. She heard the cows and their calves calling for each other as the trailer disappeared up the track. As evening fell, she heard the mother cows still calling for their young and she realised that they could feel grief, sadness and loss just as humans do.

She asked Tommy how he could bear to take the calves away, but he told her it was part of the job – and anyhow, she loved steak and leather boots, so she shouldn't complain. After that, Renee started to read and watch everything she could about veganism. Then, on 31 October 2014, at a Halloween dinner with Tommy's family, a plate of beef stew was placed in front of her and she made her decision. She could no longer eat the animals she loved. She decided to become a vegan.

Not long afterwards, Renee secretly started a blog called 'Vegan Journal of a Rancher's Wife' to share her experiences and connect with other vegans all around the world. Meanwhile, Tommy and Renee's arguments about the red trailer grew fiercer and more frequent. Tommy loved Renee, and he knew she would never change her mind about the cows. He would have to stop farming cattle. During one heated argument, Tommy announced he was going to sell the whole herd. Renee asked him how much he could get for the cows and, never believing she could get the money together, he offered her a deal: if she wanted to buy the herd, he would sell it to her for $30,000.

Tommy didn't know that Renee was dreaming of transforming the ranch into a farm animal sanctuary, to rescue cows and other animals from the dinner plate. Donations poured in from animal lovers all over the world who'd read her blog and been touched by her story. In under four months, she managed to raise over $36,000.

Tommy kept his promise and sold her the cows. In February 2015, his ranch became Rowdy Girl Sanctuary, named after the first calf Renee had fallen in love with. Now he works with his wife running the sanctuary, and he has become a vegan too. At first he claimed that it was for his health and the environment, but Renee says he loves their cows as much as if they were his children.

Over the next three years, the sanctuary became home to many other animals, as well as the cows. There's Gizmo, an affectionate pink and black hog raised by a farming student who could not face sending her to auction to be sold for meat. Pepper is a pet goat whose owner died. There's Roobadoo, the chestnut mustang horse with one blue eye and one brown eye brought in by Renee's niece. And a calf, Harvey, who they found sheltering in someone's garden after the flood. Ducks have their place here too, along with a dozen chickens – some rescued from a cockfighting ring and others from a factory farm which closed.

The sanctuary is a charity and Renee has to work hard to raise donations to pay for the animals' food, bedding, vets' bills and all the other things it needs to operate. Staff and volunteers now work there too. As well as looking after the animals, Renee and Tommy also give advice and support to other ranchers who want to leave cattle farming and change to new, greener businesses, like generating wind and solar energy. They are currently helping one ex-rancher convert his ranch to a mushroom farm. They aim to teach people about veganism through the way they live their life, rather than by telling them how to live, and many of their friends have become vegans too.

After Hurricane Harvey, Renee and Tommy eventually returned to the sanctuary with their animals. It had taken months of expensive work to repair the damage. They are planning to sell the ranch and move to a new location less likely to flood, so that they can focus on their mission of rescuing animals and letting them live out their lives in peace, and transforming the business of ranching in America. But in the meantime there is lots of work to do.

Looking out on to wrecked fences, scattered debris and damaged chicken coops left by the hurricane, Renee knows that as climate change becomes a reality, there will be many more events like these. She hopes that people will urgently rethink the food on their plates. Not just for the animals, but for the environment, and the future of the world we all share.

YIN
YUZHEN

"I PLANT TREES NOT MERELY FOR MYSELF, BUT FOR THE FUTURE GENERATIONS."

YIN YUZHEN

THE WOMAN
WHO FOUGHT
THE DESERT

The wind battered Yuzhen and knocked her to the ground. She grabbed the spade she had dropped and used it to pull herself up. The air was full of swirling sand that filled her nostrils and stung her eyes. The desert had all but disappeared in a brown haze, but she could just about make out the doorway 20 metres ahead. Struggling to stand, she staggered through the storm until she was at her front door and then banged on it, shouting above the howling gale. Her husband flung the door open and, with a look of relief on his face, pulled her inside.

It was 1986, and 20-year-old Yin Yuzhen had been

caught in a sandstorm while planting trees near her home in Jinbei Tang, Wushenqi in northern China. Yuzhen lived on the edge of the Mu Us Desert – a wild, desolate place of endless sand. Aged just 19, she had moved there from neighbouring Shaanxi province after an arranged marriage to her husband, Bai Wanxiang, who had grown up in Jinbei Tang. It was the first time Yuzhen had left her home village, a place she had always loved for its green fields and wild flowers, and she had been shocked to find that her new home was a dwelling in the desert, dug out of a slope, half buried in the sand. Yuzhen had to bend over to go inside, where the floor was carpeted with grass and deadwood.

Yuzhen had never experienced such a hostile environment. On sunny days, the shining sand hurt her eyes, while on others the wind was so strong she was afraid it would blow her away. Sandstorms could last for a whole month and there was the constant threat of dunes engulfing their home. Every day, after the winds had stopped, Yuzhen and her husband would have to shovel away the hard-packed sand from outside their door so their house would not be buried as some other homes had been. Desertification – where fertile land becomes desert – is a huge problem in China and all over the world. Caused largely by global warming and over-grazing of farm animals, it reduces the land on which crops can be grown for food. In China, it also causes dangerous clouds of dust to drift into neighbouring countries like Japan and Korea, causing many deaths due to the pollution picked up along the way – a phenomenon called 'Asian Dust'.

It was a lonely life for Yuzhen. Their nearest neighbours lived 10 kilometres away, so she might have no visitors for weeks. Wanxiang was often away during the day, travelling on foot to the next village to do labouring work. When Yuzhen travelled to see her parents, she found it terrifying because there was no protection from the blistering sun and sandstorms. She wished that there were trees along the route where she could rest in the shade. When she returned home to Wanxiang, she worried constantly about the threat of the shifting dunes.

Yuzhen's mother had taught her to be strong and to do what she could to help herself. She was determined to do something to stop the desert and make a better environment to live in. As a way of overcoming her loneliness, and desperate to do her best to protect her home, Yuzhen decided to plant trees.

That first autumn, when she went to visit her parents, she returned with two saplings which she planted next to the well she and Wanxiang had dug. She tended them carefully every day and, when spring arrived, was delighted to see that they had survived the winter. This made her determined to plant more. Wanxiang wanted to make his new wife happy, but they were very poor and had no money so he sold their goat to buy 600 saplings. Yuzhen planted these around their home, scrambling over the gleaming dunes carrying her spade and bundles of saplings. She would carefully dig holes for them in the sand, and then bring two buckets of water from the well, hanging them from a pole on her shoulders. As she dug, planted and watered, she sang songs about the desert and from her childhood in Shaanxi.

But Yuzhen and her husband knew nothing about growing trees, and of the first 600, only 10 saplings survived the brutal conditions of drought, heat, wind and frost. People laughed at them for their wasted efforts, but Yuzhen saw a reason to hope rather than despair – these 10 proved that trees *could* survive in the desert.

Within a couple of years of being married, Yuzhen and Wanxiang had built themselves a sturdy mud-brick hut to replace their desert shack. They then devoted all of their energy and any spare money to planting more trees. Wanxiang even took extra labouring jobs in nearby villages and towns, asking for saplings instead of wages. The area of green began to grow around their home, but there were still setbacks. One time, Yuzhen and her husband bought 5,000 poplar saplings from a faraway nursery, bringing them home on the back of two cows, but no sooner had they been planted than the saplings were swept away by a sandstorm. Yuzhen learned that Mongolian pine grew better in the desert and she nurtured the baby trees close to her home before planting them out in the desert. She also learned that it was best to stabilise the land first by planting shrubs, like sage brush and sand willow, which held the water in the sand and stopped it blowing away. But once she planted thousands of willows, only to see them carried away by the wind. Despite these failures, Yuzhen was never deterred. She refused to let the desert beat her.

One day while working in Erlinchuan, Wanxiang learned that the government had given the village 50,000 saplings to plant to try to hold back the desert and dunes. Most of the villagers thought this was a waste of time and the saplings lay unplanted. Wanxiang asked if he could have them and was delighted when the village officials agreed. The next morning, Yuzhen and Wanxiang left their home at 3 a.m. to make the 6-hour round trip to Erlinchuan, returning with bundles of saplings on their backs. They went back and forth for over 20 days until they'd collected all the trees. Over the following months, they planted them out, often working late into the night. That year, they were lucky to have some good periods of rain and, miraculously, half of the saplings survived and started to grow into strong trees. They named them 'Yin's Forest'.

When Yuzhen and Wanxiang became parents, their young children liked to help care for the trees and often begged to hear songs and stories about the desert. Yuzhen and Wanxiang found that the trees not only helped shelter their home from the winds, but also improved the soil so that they could grow food and keep some animals. As the dunes stopped advancing towards their house, wildlife arrived too. Yuzhen now noticed birds, foxes and rabbits where there had been none before.

As the forest grew around Yuzhen's home, people stopped laughing at her and began to help her to plant trees instead. News of 'Yin's Forest' spread, and around 15 years after she and Wanxiang had planted their first saplings, TV news reporters came to see them. Government officials soon followed and offered them more plants, money and help. A road was built to their home and they were connected to the electricity supply. Yuzhen's work was held up as an example for other regions in China to follow.

Over the last 30 years, Yuzhen has planted a million trees in around 70,000 hectares of desert – the area of 50,000 football pitches. Her small village is unrecognisable from the one she saw the day she first arrived; the endless sand has been transformed into a green oasis, with trees as far as the eye can see. There are fruit orchards, fields of wheat and colourful meadows of flowers. Cows and sheep graze contentedly and wild roosters peck the ground. Inspired by Yuzhen's success, other families from the area began to plant saplings too, and today more than 240 families have tree plantations around their homes.

Now the mother of four children, Yuzhen is also an entrepreneur. The land that she once battled is now a source of income for her family and many others in the area. She runs her own company and has created an ecological park with a sapling cultivation centre. Visitors travel from afar to see this miracle in the desert, and to learn Yuzhen's methods of fighting desertification. She has her own offices to manage the forest and nursery, while in a large meeting hall people can enjoy the organic fruit and vegetables grown on Yuzhen's land – including watermelons, pears, peaches, corn and potatoes – which Yin sells through her company *Mohai*, or 'desert ocean'.

Her home – no longer a mud-brick hut but a multistorey house – is like a small museum with walls covered in awards and certificates. The girl who had never left her village before moving to the desert has since travelled all over the world to give speeches about her work in stopping desertification. In 2005, she was nominated for the Nobel Peace Prize and she has won other international prizes, including the 2010 GAIA Prize for the environment, and the 2013 Somazzi Prize, for outstanding services to the advancement of women.

Decades after she first dreamed of transforming her desert home into a sea of green, Yuzhen still plants trees, but today volunteers from all over the world come to help her. Yuzhen no longer fights the desert. She has come to accept and love what she once hated. She knows that, although desolate, if treated well the desert can be a source of natural riches. The many trees she has planted feel like her children.

Friends have told Yuzhen that she can rest now, but she is continuing her work for the sake of her descendants and for the people across the globe who are facing the same huge issue. We may be from different countries but we share one Earth, and in the fight against desertification, as with all environmental problems, we are stronger when we fight it together.

MELATI AND ISABEL WIJSEN

MELATI AND ISABEL WIJSEN

THE SISTERS
WAVING BYE-BYE
TO PLASTIC BAGS

Melati and Isabel grabbed their towels and sprinted from the house into the rice paddies. The path led them past fields of gleaming water and bright green shoots, then into the jungle. Birds called from the treetops and thickets of bamboo. Minutes later they emerged on to the beach. There was no one around. Dropping their things on the sand, the sisters dashed down to the water and threw themselves into the turquoise waves, whooping with joy. It was Saturday so they had all morning to play. Isabel rolled on to her back while Melati started to swim across the bay. But Melati's heart suddenly sank when she saw plastic bottles, bags and bits of plastic floating in the water.

It was 2013. Twelve-year-old Melati Wijsen and her 10-year-old sister, Isabel, were in the bay near their home in Bali. The island is one of 17,508 that make up the country of Indonesia and is hugely popular with holidaymakers. Recently this tropical paradise had faced huge issues with plastic pollution. It was everywhere the girls went: piled on roadsides, blocking drains and clogging rivers which then carried it into the sea. It was strewn on the beach when they hung out with friends. Indonesia is the world's second biggest source of ocean plastic (after China). It is killing and endangering sea life and reaching people's dinner plates through the fish that eat it. The girls were upset and angry that their beautiful island home was being strangled by plastic.

The girls had always felt a deep connection to Bali's jungle, mountains and sea. When they were small, their dad sparked their love of nature. He taught them to dance in the rain and paint their faces with mud and told them Indonesian tales about people and nature. They looked up to their mum too; she taught them to work hard, be kind and do what they felt was right. The sisters were best friends, playing outside and building treehouses in the village, but developed different interests. Melati was the quieter of the two and enjoyed reading and writing. Meanwhile, Isabel was more sociable with a passion for dancing, singing and acting. Both loved going to Bali's Green School, where the teaching had a strong focus on the environment.

It was their school that inspired the sisters to become youth activists. One morning they had a lesson about people who had changed the world, including Nelson Mandela and Martin Luther King, Jr, and went home that day wondering what *they* could do to help their community. Then the answer struck them. Of course! They would try to solve the plastic pollution problem. They did some research and found that many countries had banned plastic bags, so why not Bali?

The girls recruited six of their friends and started a campaign to ban plastic bags from the island and persuade people to stop littering. They named it Bye Bye Plastic Bags. The first thing the team did was set up an online petition asking the Governor of Bali to support the ban. Within a day they had 6,000 signatures, increasing over the following months to 77,000. To boost numbers, they went to Bali airport, where they eventually persuaded the manager to allow them in to collect another 10,000 signatures.

Alongside the petition, the friends set up information

booths in local markets and organised beach clean-ups. Many other students started to join in, and the team – who called themselves the Bye Bye Plastic Bags Crew – decided to work with a nearby village, Desa Pererenan, to show what a plastic-bag-free Bali might look like. They talked to shopkeepers about the hazards of plastic waste and gave them weekly deliveries of bags made out of cotton to hand out instead of plastic ones. They also created an education booklet about plastic pollution for the primary school.

After a year, the petition had nearly 90,000 signatures and Desa Pererenan village had reduced its plastic bag usage by over 60 per cent. However, Bali's Governor still had not responded to the sisters' request for a ban. In autumn 2014, on a trip to India, they visited the National Gandhi Museum, where they learned about how he reached his goal for change in society by starting a hunger strike. Melati and Isabel wondered whether they might stage their own version of this action. They decided to fast between sunrise and sunset to get publicity for their request. News of their protest spread quickly and the next day the Governor sent a car to collect the girls from school. After meeting them, he signed an agreement to work towards a plastic-bag-free Bali.

The success of their petition had demonstrated that the people of Bali supported their campaign. Now the sisters wanted to involve businesses too, so they launched the 'One Island One Voice' campaign. This invited shops, hotels and restaurants to publicly commit to reducing their own plastic use, and to display the campaign sticker in their window. In June 2015, Bali's government announced that plastic bags would be banned by 2018, and that July, Bali airport banned them too.

The girls loved bringing together young people and seeing them take action and make decisions for themselves, but they also enjoyed taking the lead. This meant being the ones to talk to government staff – something they found difficult at first – and sometimes the sisters missed lessons to attend meetings about changing the laws in Bali relating to plastic bag use. For this, they started working with an environmental lawyer, Sarah Waddell. Their school supported them by allowing them time away, as long as they kept up with their studies.

From early on, the girls had found the most important skill was communicating well. They were regularly asked to speak at schools and community events, but in September 2015 they were given the chance to bring their message to a much bigger audience when they were invited to give a TED talk in London about their campaign. They were excited and rehearsed many times, both together and alone in front of the mirror. The talk was a huge success.

On returning from London, they were contacted by young people from all over the world who had watched their talk and wanted to start their own Bye Bye Plastic Bags campaign. In Bali, their own crew had grown to over 30 young volunteers from across Bali. Based on their experiences, the team created a starter kit for other BBPB groups to use. The youth campaign had gone global.

In February 2017, the Bali crew organised the island's biggest ever beach clean-up, which attracted 12,000 people across 55 locations on the island and collected 43 tonnes of waste. Meanwhile, around their school lessons, the girls were still pushing the Government to meet their commitment of banning plastic bags by the end of the year, which they were frustrated to realise was now unlikely to happen. With the support of their lawyer, they demonstrated that the Bali Government had the legal powers to charge for plastic bag use, although the Government argued that they needed the Indonesian Government to change the law first.

The Bali Government failed to ban plastic bags by the 2018 target. In fact, in January 2018 the pollution problem was so bad that the island declared a 'Garbage Emergency' on its most popular tourist beaches. Here sunbathers lay on golden sand strewn with food packaging and bags, while surfers bobbing behind the waves dodged waste flushed out from rivers or brought in by swirling currents. That month, officials employed 700 cleaners with 35 trucks to remove up to 100 tonnes of debris each day to a nearby landfill site.

The girls were deeply disappointed, but continued campaigning and started new green initiatives, including a project teaching school groups to make river booms – special nets that trap plastic in a river and stop it washing out to sea. Finally, in December 2018, the Bali Government announced that single-use plastics – including straws, bags, cups, bottles and cup lids – would be banned from the island from July 2019. After six years of campaigning, Melati and Isabel were thrilled to finally have the result they had been working so hard for, and today these plastic items cannot be used in Bali.

The sisters have won many awards, including TIME magazine's 2019 Teens of the Year and Forbes Magazine's Most Inspiring Women. Their TED talk has been watched over 1.5 million times online, and they have spoken at schools and events all over the world, and have even addressed world leaders. Today, Bye Bye Plastic Bags is a global youth-led movement, with 45 teams from Mexico to Japan, and Nigeria to the UK.

The sisters have also begun to look for other ways to support their community. When they were campaigning against plastic bags, they were often asked what people could use instead. Melati had an idea for how to answer that question while helping women on the island learn new skills and earn money. After getting some donated sewing machines, she set up the Mountain Mamas project in a hill village near her home. Here women learn to sew bags using fabric recycled from old clothing, sheets and towels, and make paper carrier bags from newspapers and magazines. The women are paid for each bag they make, and the bags are sold through retailers all over Bali, with half the profits from each one going back into the village to pay for health and education projects.

Melati, now 18, became a full-time activist after graduating from high school a year early. Meanwhile 16-year-old Isabel is working hard to finish her studies and, while still committed to her activism, she also dreams of a future in dance and performance.

Melati and Isabel have achieved their goal to protect their island from plastic, but now they have an even bigger mission: empowering young people to become change-makers through a new project called Youthtopia. They think young people should start working *now* for the world they want to be part of. As they put it: young people may only be 25 per cent of the population, but they are 100 per cent of the future. These change-making sisters are living proof that you're never too young to take a stand – and make a difference.

SIR DAVID ATTENBOROUGH

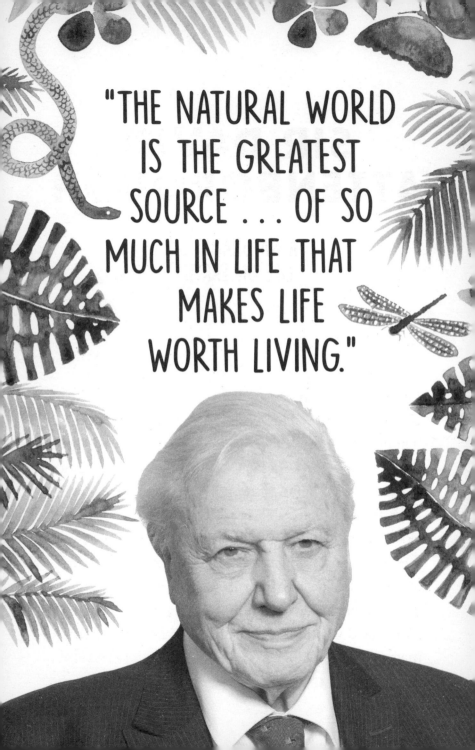

"THE NATURAL WORLD
IS THE GREATEST
SOURCE ... OF SO
MUCH IN LIFE THAT
MAKES LIFE
WORTH LIVING."

SIR DAVID ATTENBOROUGH

A NATURALIST'S LIFE ON EARTH

David was mesmerised. The reef looked like an underwater city. The coral was teeming with life. Thousands of fish of every colour swam in brightly coloured shoals – metallic blues, vivid yellows and glowing pinks. Behind him, the pilot carefully steered their three-person submarine. David pressed his face closer to the window. Around the coral he spotted sea anemones and orange and white clown fish browsing for food. Beside him, the cameraman was filming a large green turtle swimming slowly towards them. This place was just as David remembered: the most magical on the planet.

It was 2015, and 88-year-old TV presenter and writer David Attenborough was visiting the Great Barrier Reef. The reef stretches for 2,300 kilometres off the north-eastern coast of Australia, and is actually over 2,500 individual coral reefs and 900 coral islands. It is the largest living structure on Earth, a unique ecosystem – or natural environment – that is home to thousands of species of marine life. It had been almost 60 years since his first visit, in 1957, when he had dived in parts of the reef never before seen on television. But his return here was tinged with sadness. This special place was under threat.

David was born in 1926. He was full of curiosity as a boy and loved to ride his bike into the countryside near his home in Leicester to search for fossils. He always hoped to crack open a rock to reveal a creature no one else had seen in 140 million years. His dad – the head of a university – nurtured his curiosity by encouraging him to find things out from books. His mum was a specialist in languages and a suffragette who had campaigned for women to be allowed to vote. David had two brothers and when he was 14, just before the Second World War broke out, two Jewish refugee sisters from Germany also joined their family.

David was always fascinated by how the natural

world works. After the war, he studied natural sciences at university, specialising in zoology – the branch of biology that studies the animal kingdom. He then spent two years in the navy, hoping to travel around the world, but only got as far as Wales and Scotland. When he returned to civilian life, he got married and started working for a publisher of science books. He found this boring, so he applied for a job making radio programmes for the BBC. He was turned down, but offered a position as a producer making TV programmes instead. Most people then, including David, did not even own a TV set, but he accepted the job.

As a producer, David made all sorts of programmes, from dramas to quiz shows. Inspired by his love of wildlife, he created a series called *Zoo Quest*, where he travelled around the world with experts to film and capture animals for London Zoo, an idea that feels shocking today but which was very popular at that time. David's on-screen career began when the presenter of the programme fell ill and he stepped in. By this time, David and his wife, Jane, had a son and daughter. David's work sometimes made things hard for the family as he spent a lot of time away filming.

In 1962, inspired by the animals he had seen and the people he had met, David returned to university to study social anthropology. He learned about human societies, what people believe and how they live together. But in 1965, before he had finished his studies, he was offered a job running a new TV channel, BBC Two, and soon he was in charge of all BBC programmes. Although he was good at his job he was no longer doing what he loved best, so in 1972 he returned to making wildlife films.

For a long time, David had dreamed of making a series about how life developed on our planet. And in 1979, after three years of filming, *Life on Earth* was screened. 500 million people around the world watched its 13 episodes. Attitudes had changed to wildlife programmes and instead of capturing animals they were now filmed in their natural environments. One of the most memorable moments was when David sat amongst a group of mountain gorillas in Rwanda. The female gorilla put her hands on his head and opened his mouth to look inside. Meanwhile one of her baby gorillas sat on his lap while another tried to take off his boots. As David looked into the female gorilla's eyes, he felt a deep connection with her and sensed how similar these wonderful animals are to humans. It was one of the most important moments of his life.

Over the 40 years that followed, David continued

to bring the wonders of nature into people's homes. Viewers saw rare snow leopards high in the Himalayan mountains, millions of red crabs marching from the forest to the sea, a baby iguana chased by snakes, an Australian Lyrebird mimicking the sound of a camera shutter, chainsaw and car alarm, and an enormous rainforest flower that smelled of rotting fish.

It was only in 2002, aged 75 and after decades of filming, that David saw a blue whale for the first time when one of these magnificent creatures – they are the largest on the planet – surfaced next to his boat. With unforgettable moments like this, his career has given him great joy, but more recently he has felt a terrible sense of loss. It has become clear to David that one species is destroying the natural world he cherishes: humans.

Twenty thousand years ago there were fewer than a million people on the planet, all living as hunter-gatherers. When David started his career, the world's human population was 2.5 billion. In his lifetime, he has seen that treble to 7.7 billion, and it is predicted to reach nine billion by around 2030. Humans, through our demand for land and resources, have driven many species to extinction. Today, humans and the animals we raise for food make up 96 per cent of all mammals and 70 per cent of all birds on Earth.

Because of human actions, climate change threatens the world's ecosystems. David remembers returning to a glacier in South Georgia to find it had disappeared. On his visit to the Great Barrier Reef, he was devastated to see that vast areas were white with 'coral bleaching', which is where the coral dies due to warming oceans and seawater becoming more acidic from pollution. If global temperatures rise by just two degrees Celsius, scientists predict that all the planet's coral reefs will die.

For David, whether it's a coral reef or an English woodland, the loss of biodiversity – or variety in plant and animal life – is both a tragedy and one of the biggest problems faced by humankind. We are part of the natural world and depend on it for every breath of air and every mouthful of food. As we shift the balance of nature, the world no longer works as it should and our own existence is threatened.

Never before has one species been responsible for the fate of the whole planet. Today, according to the United Nations, more than 50 per cent of people live in urban areas. Humans have never been more disconnected from nature, yet never have our actions had more impact upon it. David hopes his programmes show why the natural world should be protected and how we can do that. He didn't start out to be a campaigner – he was just doing a job he loved – but in recent years this has meant telling everyone about the destruction he witnesses.

Perhaps the most powerful example was from *Blue Planet II*, shown in 2017, which explores the Earth's oceans. This was so popular around the world that it even slowed down internet speeds in China as 80 million people downloaded it. As expected, the series showed incredible marine life, but what people remember most is seeing the devastating impact of plastic in our oceans: a dolphin playing with a plastic bag, an albatross chick that had died after swallowing a plastic toothpick and pilot whales killed by plastic pollution.

Viewers were shocked and countless individuals and organisations were moved to take action. The BBC declared it would ban single-use plastics by 2020 and other businesses followed their example. In 2019, the Glastonbury Festival went plastic-free and, to the delight of festival-goers of all ages, David made a surprise appearance onstage to thank the crowds there.

David has gained global recognition for his achievements and was honoured with a knighthood in 1985. At least 20 species, both living and extinct, have been named after Sir David (as he can now be called), from grasshoppers and butterflies to lizards and a lion, and in 2017 a new constellation of stars in the shape of a blue whale was named the 'Attenborough'. His many fans include Prince William and Barack Obama, both of whom have interviewed him. And in a recent poll he was voted the most trusted celebrity in the UK. He thinks he is the luckiest man in the world and has never thought of retiring.

Despite the damage inflicted on the natural world, David remains hopeful. Human population growth is slowing and can be stopped if we lift people out of poverty, ensure girls are able to go to school and invest in women's rights. If this can be done, people will naturally start to have smaller families. And, he says, if we focus on four areas – renewable energy, the food we grow and eat, protecting our oceans and nurturing our wild spaces and their plant and animal life – then humans can find a way to live in balance with nature and we can both thrive.

David was encouraged when countries came together in 2015 to sign the Paris Agreement to limit global warming, but the thing that gives him most hope is seeing young people demanding action against climate change, sparked by Greta Thunberg's protest. It's clear to him that his grandchildren's generation understand the issues and will fight hard for the planet they will inherit.

At heart, David's concern is not about just one species. All the plants and animals that exist today are the result of 3.5 billion years of evolution and he is horrified that one generation of humans could destroy it all. He believes we have no choice but to act to save the natural world – and not just because it's good for humans, but simply because it's the right thing to do. The work and wisdom of this inspirational man has taught us so much through the years, but the need for urgent action must be his most important lesson yet.

CONCLUSION

YOU TOO CAN CHANGE THE WORLD

I hope you enjoyed meeting these *Earth Heroes* as much as I did. I was inspired and humbled to hear what they achieved, often against the odds. Writing their stories filled me with mixed emotions: anger that countries that have contributed least to climate change are worst affected by it; sadness at the ongoing loss of our wonderful natural world; gratitude that these people, and many others like them, are working tirelessly for our planet; and joy and hope on seeing the impact they have had. Everything I've learned has made me more determined to look for ways that I can help too.

I'd like to thank the people who generously made

time to talk to me or answer questions on email: Bittu Sahgal, David Turton (Andrew's big brother), Doug Smith, Isabel Soares, Isatou Ceesay, Mohammed Rezwan, Pete Ceglinski and Rok Rozman. Their contributions really helped me get to the heart of their incredible stories, but for those I wasn't able to speak to I've had to imagine how it might have felt to walk in their shoes. If you'd like to know more about the people in this book, many have their own websites and some, such as William Kamkwamba and Sheila Watt-Cloutier, have written autobiographies. Search online for more details.

There are so many other amazing activists I could have included, it's impossible to list them all. From 11-year-old Yola Mgogwana spreading the environmental message in her community in South Africa, to 11-year-old Finlay Pringle campaigning against sharks in captivity and his 10-year-old sister Ella organising anti-whaling marches in Scotland. From teen activist and hip-hop artist Xiuhtezcatl Martinez, one of 21 young people suing President Trump for failing to act against climate change, to Boyan Slat, the Dutch inventor creating technology to clean up the Great Pacific Garbage Patch. There are change-makers all around you.

There is no one solution to the environmental crisis, and there is much to do. While I've written about individual *Earth Heroes*, they would probably be the first to say that they only achieved what they did with the support and hard work of friends, colleagues and countless others. If we look back in history, most positive change in the world happens when people come together to fight for issues that they care about.

But our individual actions make a difference too. Small steps are just as important as big ones – and everyone can demand change. The task may seem overwhelming sometimes, but we need to play our part. As Greta Thunberg says, "The one thing we need more than hope is action. Once we start to act, hope is everywhere."

And as well as taking care of nature, take time to enjoy it too. Be amazed by swallows flying thousands of miles from Africa each spring to return to the same nests, be astonished at how a tiny caterpillar can transform into a beautiful butterfly, and be grateful for the miracle of trees absorbing carbon and producing life-giving oxygen. And last but not least, be proud of how humans, who are just as much part of nature as any other species, have created music, poetry, art, technology and medicine. We have achieved incredible things, and now we need to fight for the planet we love.

The future is ours for the making. You too can change the world.

Lily Dyu

September 2019

PICTURE CREDITS

Amelia Telford © Tracey Nearmy / Getty Images – p48
Andrew Turton and Pete Ceglinski © Seabin – p180
Bittu Sahgal © Archive PL / Alamy Stock Photo – p156
Chewang Norphel © Emma Stoner / Alamy Stock Photo – p132
David Attenborough © Lev Radin / Shutterstock – p224
Doug Smith © William Campbell / Getty Images – p84
Ellen MacArthur © Neale Haynes / Getty Images – p144
Greta Thunberg © Daniele Cossu / Shutterstock – p2
Isabel Soares © Fruta Feia   p60
Isatou Ceesay © Luke Duggleby – p120
Marina Silva © Victor Moriyama / Getty Images – p96
Melati and Isabel Wijsen © Andrew Wyman – p212
Mohammed Rezwan © Abir Abdullah / Shidhulai Swanirvar Sangstha – p14
Renee King-Sonnen © Marie D. De Jesús – p192
Rok Rozman © Jan Pirnat / Balkan River Defence – p36

Sheila Watt-Cloutier © David Wolff – Patrick / Redferns Getty Images – p168

Stella McCartney © Lev Radin / Shutterstock – p26

William Kamkwamba © Lucas Oleniuk / Getty Images – p72

Yin Yuzhen © Maren Haartje / PeaceWomen Across the Globe – p202

Yvon Chouinard © Al Seib / Getty Images – p108

QUOTE CREDITS

Amelia Telford: *It's Time For Solidarity, Not Sympathy* by Amelia Telford www.huffingtonpost.com.au/amelia-telford/climate-change-and-forced_b_8658700.html (2015) – p48

Andrew Turton and Pete Ceglinski: *About Us* © The Seabin Project seabinproject.com/about-us/our-purpose/ (2019) – p180

Bittu Sahgal: Interview with Lily Dyu, *Earth Heroes* (2019) and interview with Tina Dastur, *Bittu Sahgal on Restoring the Balance Between Man and Nature* www.vervemagazine.in/people/bittu-sahgal-on-restoring-the-balance-between-man-and-nature (2019) – iv and p156

Chewang Norphel: Interview with Ieva Maniusyte, Chewang Norphel, *Ice Man's Dams in the Himalayas* climateheroes.org/heroes/chewang-norphel-ice-mans-dams-himalayas/ (2014) – p132

David Attenborough: www.independent.co.uk/arts-entertainment/tv/news/david-attenborough-best-quotes-birthday-a7724216.html (2017) and inews.co.uk/culture/television/david-attenborough-quotes-93rd-birthday/ (2019) – p224

Doug Smith: Interview with Lily Dyu, *Earth Heroes* (2019) – p84

Ellen MacArthur: *The Surprising Thing I Learned Sailing Solo Around the World* by Ellen MacArthur TEDTalk (2015) – p144

Greta Thunberg: *Extinction Rebellion Speech Outside Parliament Square* by Greta Thunberg www.facebook.com/ExtinctionRebellion/videos/greta-thunberg-full-speech-at-parliament-square/2215034952158269/ (2019) – p2, jacket and back of hardcover and *The Disarming Case to Act Right Now on Climate Change* by Greta Thunberg, TEDxStockholm (2018) – p237

Isabel Soares: *Company motto* © Fruta Feia frutafeia.pt/en/the-project (2019) – p60

Isatou Ceesay: *Queen of Recycling in the Gambia*, a film by Max Riché (2015) vimeo.com/144419980 – p120

Marina Silva: Translated from Portuguese, *Children Give the Cry of the Future* by Marina Silva www.poder360.com.br/opiniao/internacional/as-criancas-dao-o-grito-do-futuro-escreve-marina-silva/ (2019) – p96